HERO TALES

VOLUME IV

DAVE & NETA
JACKSON

BETHANY HOUSE PUBLISHERS
MINNEAPOLIS, MINNESOTA 55438

Books by Dave and Neta Jackson

Hero Tales: A Family Treasury of True Stories
From the Lives of Christian Heroes (Volumes I, II, III, and IV)

Trailblazer Books

William & Catherine Booth • *Kidnapped by River Rats*
Charles Loring Brace • *Roundup of the Street Rovers*
Governor William Bradford • *The Mayflower Secret*
John Bunyan • *Traitor in the Tower*
Amy Carmichael • *The Hidden Jewel*
George Washington Carver • *The Forty-Acre Swindle*
Maude Cary • *Risking the Forbidden Game*
Frederick Douglass • *Caught in the Rebel Camp*
Elizabeth Fry • *The Thieves of Tyburn Square*
Chief Spokane Garry • *Exiled to the Red River*
Barbrooke Grubb • *Ambushed in Jaguar Swamp*
Adoniram & Ann Judson • *Imprisoned in the Golden City*
David Livingstone • *Escape from the Slave Traders*
Martin Luther • *Spy for the Night Riders*
Samuel Morris • *Quest for the Lost Prince*
George Müller • *The Bandit of Ashley Downs*
John Newton • *The Runaway's Revenge*
Florence Nightingale • *The Drummer Boy's Battle*
John G. Paton • *Sinking the Dayspring*
William Penn • *Hostage on the Nighthawk*
Nate Saint • *The Fate of the Yellow Woodbee*
Mary Slessor • *Trial by Poison*
Hudson Taylor • *Shanghaied to China*
Harriet Tubman • *Listen for the Whippoorwill*
William Tyndale • *The Queen's Smuggler*
John Wesley • *The Chimney Sweep's Ransom*

Hero Tales, Volume IV: A Family Treasury of True Stories From the Lives of Christian Heroes
Copyright © 2001
Dave and Neta Jackson

Cover design by Josh Madison
Interior illustrations by Toni Auble

Published by Bethany House Publishers
11400 Hampshire Avenue South
Bloomington, Minnesota 55438
www.bethanyhouse.com

Bethany House Publishers is a division of
Baker Publishing Group, Grand Rapids, Michigan.

Printed in the United States of America

ISBN 0-7642-0078-X (Volume I)
ISBN 0-7642-0079-8 (Volume II)
ISBN 0-7642-0080-1 (Volume III)
ISBN 0-7642-0081-X (Volume IV)

Library of Congress Cataloging-in-Publication Data

Jackson, Dave.
    Hero tales: a family treasury of true stories from the lives of Christian heroes / Dave and Neta Jackson.
        p. cm.
    Summary: Presents biographies of fifteen missionaries, evangelists, and other Christian heroes who worked courageously to share the Gospel with others.

    1. Christian biography—Juvenile literature. 2. Missionaries—Biography—Juvenile literature.
[1. Christian biography. 2. Missionaries.] I. Jackson, Neta. II. Title.
BR1704.J33   1996
270′092′2—dc20   96-25230
[B]   CIP
                                                                                  AC

To

Sabrina, Kelley, and Ricky Byrdsong—
who already know their parents are heroes.

CONTENTS ✺

RICKY & SHERIALYN BYRDSONG

Coaching Kids in the Game of Life

Ricky Byrdsong was only fifteen when he met Sherialyn Kelley on a blind date on Christmas Day, 1972. The six-foot-six basketball player was smitten with the athletic Sherialyn, who was smart as well as pretty. The high school sweethearts both graduated from Iowa State University and were married on October 6, 1979.

Ricky started coaching college ball immediately after graduation in 1978. His nineteen-year coaching career took him finally to Northwestern University in Evanston, Illinois, as head basketball coach.

Sherialyn, too, was "Coach Byrdsong" at the University of Arizona, coaching women's basketball at the same time her husband was coaching men's basketball there. When the kids came along, Sherialyn became an at-home mom but continued to coach sports at her kids' schools.

Both Ricky and Sherialyn made serious decisions as adults to live for Christ. Ricky realized there was a lot more to life than just playing basketball. Coaching became a way to teach life principles of discipline, following the rules, cooperation, a positive spirit, and learning from mistakes. Win or lose, Ricky was always a role model of integrity and a man of faith.

Meanwhile, God was using Sherialyn to coach others in worship and the study of God's Word. While Ricky was head coach at Northwestern University, Sherialyn became the praise and worship team leader at The Worship Center, a church with a vision to unite persons of many races in Christian worship

When a losing streak cost him his job at NWU, Ricky began working on a book that had been gnawing inside him—a book for parents about "coaching kids in the game of life," using sports metaphors to teach parents how to encourage and guide their children.

Then he was offered a job—not as a university basketball coach, but as vice president of community affairs for the Aon Corporation. His job description? Developing programs to help underprivileged youth reach their full potential. Speaking in schools and bringing inner-city kids to his "Not-Just-Basketball Camps," Ricky was doing what he did best—coaching kids in the game of life.

Then . . . tragedy. On July 2, 1999, while jogging in his suburban neighborhood with two of his children, Ricky was shot and killed by a young white supremacist during a two-state shooting spree. People nationwide were stunned by his murder.

Suddenly Sherialyn, only forty-two, was a widow with three preteen children. She was at a crossroad. She could give in to despair, bitterness, and self-pity . . . or she could believe that God's love is stronger than hate. In the media spotlight since her husband's murder, she has turned tragedy into triumph through public witness to her faith in God and by establishing the Ricky Byrdsong Foundation. The Foundation seeks to address the growing epidemic of violence in our society by providing opportunities for young people that instill a sense of self-worth and purpose and develop respect for others.

The torch has been passed from one Coach Byrdsong to another.

ADVOCATE
Windy-City Panhandler

~~~~~~

James Saunders sized up the tall, good-looking black man walking briskly up Wacker Drive and decided he looked like a good mark. "Got a dollar or two, mister?" he called out. Unlike some of the other panhandlers in downtown Chicago, James knew he wouldn't get snide remarks like "Get a job, buddy." Not many people could pass by the wheelchair of a double amputee without throwing *something* into his hat.

"Sure," said the tall man, digging out a five-dollar bill. "Say, losing your legs must be tough. What happened?"

James was surprised. Most people just dropped in the money and hurried off. Not many stayed to talk.

It was the first of many talks on the corner of Wacker Drive and Monroe. James told his new friend, who introduced himself as Ricky Byrdsong, that he'd been stabbed in the back at age twenty-five, which paralyzed him from the waist down. An infection in his bones took off first one leg, then the other. For the past twenty-five years he'd been in and out of hospitals, had married three times, and held piecemeal jobs.

Ricky Byrdsong told James he used to be the head basketball

coach at Northwestern University "... until I got sacked a year ago." He laughed ruefully. "Nobody would hire a coach with a losing streak. Didn't think about panhandling, though. . . . You make good money on this corner?"

James laughed in spite of himself. The tall man was obviously well-off now. Turned out that he worked across the street at the Aon Corporation—the second largest insurance broker in the world—as vice president of community affairs.

"Don't you miss coaching?" he asked his new friend.

Byrdsong grinned broadly from ear to ear. "James, I've got the greatest job in the world. They're actually *paying* me to go to schools, talk to kids about what's important in life, and run basketball camps for inner-city kids in the summer. Not *just* basketball, either. Kids come to camp to play basketball half the time; the other half we teach them computer skills, take them to work, try to give them a vision for something besides basketball." His eyes had fire in them. "I want them to know there are other options besides becoming an NBA superstar like Michael Jordan—which isn't very likely—or hustling drugs. I want kids to know there's dignity in education and hard work."

Dignity. Pride. That was hard to come by panhandling on a street corner, even though it put food in his stomach and helped pay the rent. There was something about Ricky Byrdsong that inspired James Saunders, made him want to "stand tall," get off this street corner, and do something with his life.

"Ricky, do you think you could help me get a job?" he asked one winter morning as the two men exchanged their usual hellos.

Byrdsong scratched the back of his head. "Can't promise anything, James. But I'll see what I can do."

Within a couple of days Ricky ushered James's wheelchair into the Human Resources office of the Aon Corporation. There was a job in the mailroom. Did James think he could handle it?

James could hardly believe his ears. "I'll be the best employee you've got!" he said. "I'm dependable. I'll show up here on time, even stay overtime if I need to."

"He's got *that* right!" Ricky Byrdsong chimed in. "If this guy can show up on a street corner in the Windy City every morning, rain or shine, summer or winter, without fail, you *know* he's going to show up for an inside job!"

Their laughter bounced off the walls. And James was true to his word. He didn't make as much money as he sometimes did panhandling, but Ricky Byrdsong had given him something far better: friendship and dignity.

An advocate speaks up on behalf of someone else who is often overlooked in society.

FROM GOD'S WORD:
Defend the cause of the weak and fatherless; maintain the rights of the poor and oppressed (Psalm 82:3, NIV).

LET'S TALK ABOUT IT:
1. Why would a man like Ricky Byrdsong make friends with a panhandler who "worked the corner" across from the big corporation where he worked?
2. Why is helping someone get a job more helpful than just giving someone money?
3. Is there someone you pass by every day—on the way to work or school—who needs *you* to be an advocate for him or her?

VICTORY

From Tragedy to Triumph

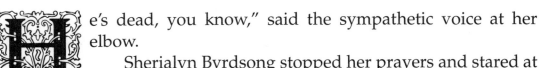

He's dead, you know," said the sympathetic voice at her elbow.

Sherialyn Byrdsong stopped her prayers and stared at the intensive-care nurse.

"Dead?" she echoed in disbelief. "Dead?" How could this be happening? Not Ricky, not her big strapping husband who was so full of life. Murdered?

The screams of her children still rang in her ears: *"Daddy's been shot!"* At 8:52 on a peaceful summer evening in their quiet neighborhood in Skokie, Illinois, a lone gunman had opened fire on her husband and children as they were coming home from a nearby park. The children were all right—traumatized, but alive—but Ricky... Ricky was dead.

The next few days were a blur. It was Fourth of July weekend, 1999. Newscasters were saying the gunman was a white supremacist shooting at over twenty-five Jews, Blacks, and Asians in a two-state spree. The shooter finally turned the gun on himself as the police closed in. Three dead—counting the shooter's suicide—and twelve wounded.

Calls of sympathy came pouring into the Byrdsong home from all over the world. Sherialyn could barely think about *why* Ricky had been shot. Just because he was *black*? It didn't make sense! Her husband was working at a job he loved, motivating kids to become all God meant for them to be. His kids needed their dad. And just two weeks earlier Ricky had heard that a publisher wanted the parenting book he was working on.

At the same time she knew why. The stronghold of evil was in a spiritual warfare with the kingdom of God, and the Evil One had scored a victory by eliminating a man who was influencing others for good, who had gotten to the place in his life where "nothing else mattered" other than living for God.

Two days after her husband's murder, Sherialyn Byrdsong held a press conference. People who watched were impressed by her poise and dignity. "The violent act that took my husband's life is yet another clarion call to our nation. . . . Wake up, America! It's time to turn back to God. . . . This is not a gun problem, it's a heart problem, and only God and reading His word can change our hearts."

In a private sharing with her church family, she said, "In the twenty years I've been a Christian, all the Scripture I've studied and all the worship songs I've ever learned were like deposits into my heart. Now I'm making withdrawals big time."

Working with Ricky's co-writers, Sherialyn Byrdsong helped oversee his book to completion, making sure that it reflected the heart of what he wanted to say to parents.[1] A lot of her energy went into establishing the Ricky Byrdsong Foundation to continue her husband's work with youth, giving them positive alternatives to a culture of violence. All three of the Byrdsong kids ran in the Ricky Byrdsong Memorial 5K Run a year after their father was killed, an event that brought together nearly two thousand people of all races pledging themselves to work against violence and hate. And on the one-year

---

[1]*Coaching Your Kids in the Game of Life* by Ricky Byrdsong with Dave and Neta Jackson (Bethany House Publishers, 2000).

anniversary of her husband's death, at a memorial celebration called "From Tragedy to Triumph," Sherialyn spoke to a gathering who worshiped together across racial and denominational lines, to praise the King of Kings and to commit themselves to let God's love be stronger than hate.

As Sherialyn worked through her grief, keeping her eyes not on her loss but on Jesus, she taught a series of Bible studies at her church, addressing the question "Is God good?" Her answer: a resounding YES. "If we understand the sovereignty of God, we'll understand it's not *about* us. It's about God!"

Some people are defeated by problems; others
understand that God has already given us victory.

FROM GOD'S WORD:
"Death is destroyed forever in victory." . . . But we thank God! He gives us the victory through our Lord Jesus Christ (1 Corinthians 15:54b, 57, NCV).

LET'S TALK ABOUT IT:
1. What do you think Sherialyn Byrdsong meant when she said that studying the Bible and singing worship songs were "deposits" in her heart, and now she was making "withdrawals" to help her through this tragedy?
2. Why do you think Sherialyn Byrdsong called the senseless murder of her husband a "wake-up call"?
3. Have you ever lost someone close to you in a tragic way? Do you sometimes wonder if God really *is* good? How can you turn loss or tragedy into triumph?

GENEROSITY
The Missing Shoes

But, Dad. . . !"

"*I said no, so don't keep asking. I'm not going to put out money for expensive athletic shoes just for a one-week basketball camp. What's wrong with your sneakers?*"

His father's words still echoed in his head as the ten-year-old boy mingled with the other kids who had signed up for Ricky Byrdsong's summer basketball camp at Northwestern University. The gym was full of black kids and white kids, kids wearing squeaky-clean athletic shoes, tossing the ball around, shootin' hoops. . . . But he didn't see anyone else wearing a yarmulke on his head.

A tall guy holding a basketball on his hip walked over to the boy. "Hi, son. I'm Coach Byrdsong. You bring any other shoes to play in?"

The boy reddened and looked down at his muddy sneakers. He shook his head. "My dad wouldn't buy me any new shoes for camp."

The coach raised his eyebrows. "Stay right there, son," he said and walked off the floor. A few minutes later he was back, jangling his car keys. "C'mon." Puzzled, the boy obediently trotted after the coach as he headed out to the parking lot. Coach Byrdsong unlocked his Jeep Cherokee and said, "Get in."

"Where we goin'?"

"To get you a pair of shoes." The coach grinned.

The boy's eyes flew wide. "Aw, no, coach. My dad wouldn't want you to do that."

"Get in, son. If you want to play ball, you gotta have good gym shoes—and they can't go outside playing in the mud."

The boy tried a few more times to tell Coach Byrdsong that his dad wasn't going to like it, but the coach cheerfully ignored him. He asked the shoe man to measure the boy's feet and fit him with a good pair of basketball shoes. Then he pulled out his wallet, paid for the shoes, and gave the bag to the boy to carry.

Back in the car, the boy tried again. "My dad will make me bring them back."

"Don't worry about it, son. I'll talk to your dad if it's a problem."

Man, those shoes felt good running up and down the basketball court. And when they took a break from doing skills and drills, the boy listened as Coach Byrdsong gave them some tips about basketball . . . and life. "What's the most important skill you can develop? A positive attitude! You got the right attitude, you're on the way to being a winner!" And "Respect! Every member of this team deserves respect. And that includes the manager and everyone else on the staff. I don't want to see any of you leaving your towel around the locker room, thinking somebody else can pick it up for you."

By the time he got home, the boy had figured out how to handle his little problem. When his dad got home from work—as CEO of a large Chicago company—the brand-new athletic shoes were safely stowed at the back of the boy's closet. They only came out in time to get smuggled to camp, then back in the closet. And when basketball camp was over, there they stayed.

A couple of years passed. It was summer again and the boy—a teenager now—was excited about the plans his family was making to celebrate July Fourth, which fell the day after Sabbath. But suddenly news was spreading like wildfire over Chicago's airwaves and newspapers: A lone gunman had opened fire on a group of Orthodox Jews walking home from Sabbath services, wounding several. Then the gunman had driven north and killed an African-American man jogging home from the park with his kids.

The man who had been shot was Coach Ricky Byrdsong.

Suddenly the teenager remembered the shoes in the back of his closet. "Dad?" he said, digging out the shoes, tears filling his eyes. "I've got something to tell you."

A spirit of generosity delights in sharing whatever we have with whoever needs it.

FROM GOD'S WORD:
You must each make up your own mind as to how much you should give. . . . For God loves the person who gives cheerfully (2 Corinthians 9:7).

LET'S TALK ABOUT IT:
1. What do you think the father's reaction was when he heard that Coach Byrdsong had bought his son basketball shoes—shoes the father easily could have afforded?
2. Why do you think Ricky Byrdsong left the basketball camp to buy shoes for one boy instead of just saying, "No shoes, no play"?
3. Brainstorm some ways you (and your family) can develop a generous spirit.

BEN CARSON

The Brain Surgeon They Called "Dummy"

"Benjamin, you're much too smart to be bringing home grades like this."

Ben Carson was sorry to disappoint his mother again, but she just didn't understand what it was like at school. He was possibly the worst fifth-grade student in the school, and his nickname was "Dummy." For Ben, a good day was when he got someone else kicked out of class rather than himself.

"I've been praying for wisdom about what to do," continued his mother, "and I think the Lord's answered my prayer. From now on, only two or three TV programs per week—"

"Per week?" howled Ben and his brother, Curtis. "What are we going to do?"

"Oh, the Lord told me that, too. From now on you're going to read two books a week and write me a report on each of them."

"But we don't have any books."

"No problem. You can catch the bus and ride right down to the Detroit Public Library, where they have more books than you can read in ten lifetimes."

At first, Ben thought his mom was cruel and heartless, but it was the beginning of the beginning for him. Even though their family had no money, between the covers of those books Ben discovered that he could go anywhere in the world, be anybody, do anything. Instead of wanting to just get out of school and work in some factory so he could buy clothes and a cool car, Ben began imagining himself as a scientist discovering all sorts of new things.

In fifth grade, he had considered himself stupid, so he acted stupid and achieved nothing. But by seventh grade, he knew that he was smart. So he behaved and achieved like a smart person. He had moved from the bottom of his class to the top, and the same students who used to call him "Dummy" were now begging him to help them with their homework.

Of course, some of them were still caught in the "stupid" trap, so instead of calling Ben "Dummy," they began calling him "Nerd" and "Poindexter" and "Uncle Tom." But Ben had caught a vision for the future and didn't let the names bother him. Instead, he said, "Let's see what I'm doing in twenty years, and let's see what you're doing in twenty years. Then we'll see who's right."

Twenty years later, at age thirty-three, Ben Carson was named chief of pediatric neurosurgery at Baltimore's Johns Hopkins Hospital, becoming the youngest U.S. doctor to hold such a position. Three years later he made worldwide headlines by leading a twenty-eight-hour operation to separate South African Siamese twins joined at the head—the first such procedure ever to succeed for both patients.

Today he performs as many as five hundred operations per year—more than twice the number done by most brain surgeons—saving the lives of children who often have no other hope.

Ben's older brother also benefited from their mother's reading plan. Today Curtis Carson is a successful engineer.

VISION
One Shiny Rock

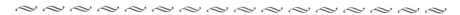

hen the teacher passed out the math quiz and Ben Carson looked at the thirty problems, his heart sank. Nothing looked familiar. He put his name at the top of the paper, guessed at a few answers, and then fiddled with his pencil until time was up. The teacher had all the students pass their papers to the person behind and then gave out the answers while the kids graded one another's papers.

The girl behind Ben handed his paper back with a big goose egg at the top—zero. He hadn't gotten even one answer right! It was what he expected, but he was tired of being laughed at as the dumbest kid in class, so when the teacher called his name for his score, he mumbled, "Nuhhhhn," hoping she wouldn't understand.

"Nine!" the teacher exclaimed. "Benjamin, you got nine right? That's wonderful. Class, can you see what Benjamin has done? Didn't I tell you that if you apply yourself you can do it?"

Nine out of thirty wasn't really very good, but for Ben it would have been a start. But the girl behind him yelled, "None, not nine! He got *none* right. Zero!"

The class burst into laughter, the teacher got angry, and Ben wished he hadn't even gotten out of bed that day.

But a little over a year later—after Ben had been "suffering" under his mother's requirement that he cut down on TV and read two books per week—a remarkable thing happened. He was sitting in science class still feeling as dumb as ever when his teacher held up a shiny black rock with sharp edges and asked the students what it was.

No one answered, not even the smartest kids in class. Ben squinted at the rock. He had just read about different kinds of rocks and had written a report for his mother. He raised his hand and said, "Obsidian."

The teacher almost didn't notice. Then he blinked. "What did you say?"

"Obsidian. That's obsidian." Ben started to shrink down into his seat thinking he'd made a fool of himself again.

"You're right! You're right, Ben!" said his amazed teacher. "This is obsidian."

Ben gained courage. "It's formed from a volcano. When lava flows down and hits water, it supercools. The elements come together, air is forced out, and the surface becomes like glass."

Suddenly he realized everyone was staring at him in amazement. It had all happened because he had been reading books. He wasn't a dummy after all!

A vision began to form in his mind. He didn't need to be a dummy if he kept on reading books—books about science, math, history, geography, social studies, literature, art, and music. They could become his ticket anywhere.

When his mom took him to the hospital clinic for checkups, Ben heard them paging, "Dr. Jones to the emergency room. Dr. Johnson. Dr. Johnson to the clinic." A vision grew in his mind: One day they'd be saying, "Dr. Carson to the operating room."

Now, as a world-famous brain surgeon, he says, "I had the same brain when I was at the bottom of the class as I had when I reached the top. It is all a matter of vision, how one sees oneself."

Vision sees what is not and knows that by faith it can be.

FROM GOD'S WORD:
This happened because Abraham believed in the God who brings . . . into existence what didn't exist before (Romans 4:17b).

LET'S TALK ABOUT IT:
1. Why did Ben mumble, "Nuhhhhn," when the teacher asked what his quiz score was?
2. How did Ben know what obsidian was?
3. What is *your* vision for what you might become or accomplish someday with God's help?

WISDOM
Crabs in a Bucket

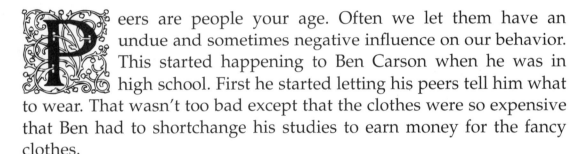**P**eers are people your age. Often we let them have an undue and sometimes negative influence on our behavior. This started happening to Ben Carson when he was in high school. First he started letting his peers tell him what to wear. That wasn't too bad except that the clothes were so expensive that Ben had to shortchange his studies to earn money for the fancy clothes.

Then his friends began suggesting that Ben wasn't "cool" if he was inside in the evenings studying. "Hey, man, what's the matter with you? It's only nine o'clock. Why aren't you outside playing basketball with us?"

Then his peers began ridiculing Ben for getting good grades. They were like crabs in a bucket. The first time Ben or anyone else began climbing up the side to get out, the others would grab him and pull him down. If they had their way, no one would escape their "bucket" of poverty and ignorance.

Ben began letting these ideas influence him. With it came a victim mentality preoccupied with "my rights." "I began to think that the world owed me something," says Ben as he looks back on those years.

"It created a bomb of anger within me, always threatening to explode if anyone crossed me.

"One day I got so angry at a friend that I lunged at him with a knife, aiming it right at his stomach. By God's grace, the knife hit his belt buckle and broke the blade without hurting him."

His friend ran off, terrified, and Ben began to shake as he realized what had almost happened. What if he had wounded or even killed his friend? He would have had to live with that guilt for the rest of his life—possibly in jail.

Ben began to understand that anger and acting out weren't making him a strong person like his peers had been saying. He was actually acting like a weak person, letting other people tell him how to act, and it had almost ruined his life. The event shook him up enough that he decided to quit letting his peers tell him what was *cool* and to start studying again.

Ben now says peers are often "P-E-E-R-S—People who Encourage Errors, Rudeness, and Stupidity. We don't want to let that happen to us. God didn't give us these incredible brains so we could go off and act like maniacs every time we think somebody is looking at us the wrong way."

Be wise! Don't let your peers pull you down like crabs in a bucket.

Wisdom will save you from evil people
and bad consequences.

FROM GOD'S WORD:
Only fools despise wisdom and discipline (Proverbs 1:7b).

LET'S TALK ABOUT IT:
1. Why are negative peers like crabs in a bucket? Why do you think some kids try to talk their friends out of studying hard?
2. If Ben's knife blade had not broken in his friend's belt buckle, how might his life have been different?
3. Tell about a time when some of your peers encouraged errors, rudeness, and stupidity. How did you respond? Why?

VICTORY
It's No Accident

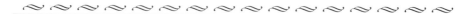

ome people think success is accidental good luck, like a prize you might win at a party. Ben Carson learned that success is a choice or, rather, the result of a series of choices.

When Ben's mother insisted that her boys quit watching so much TV and start reading books, she couldn't even read the book reports she required them to write (though they didn't know that at the time). She had come from a family with twenty-four children, where she received only a third-grade education. She got married at the age of thirteen, had two children, and then her husband abandoned the family. But she never felt sorry for herself, and she never allowed her sons to blame others or their circumstances for their problems.

She knew education was the only way her boys would triumph over their severe poverty. A choice had to be made between failure and success, being a victim or a victor, and she made that choice for them until they were old enough to make it for themselves.

In the last couple years of high school, Ben did well enough to earn a scholarship to Yale University, where he also did well. But when he entered the University of Michigan Medical School, things didn't go so smoothly, and before long his advisor actually recommended that he drop out. "There are other useful fields you might pursue," he suggested after reviewing Ben's scores.

Ben, however, refused to take the easy way out. The advisor then suggested a compromise: Go more slowly. Take four years to complete what most people do in two.

Should he take this advice? Ben went to his room and prayed. He knew he wasn't dumb, so he didn't want to accept a "dumbed down" way out of his problem. In Ben's prayer time, God reminded him of his strengths. Ben learned best from what he read. But he had the most trouble listening to lectures in classrooms. Unfortunately, at that stage of his medical training, most of the material was communicated by lecture in the classroom.

No wonder his grades weren't up to his usual high standards. So Ben made a decision: He would skip most of the lectures and spend that time and more reading medical books. The plan worked.

"If I had accepted a victim mentality," says Ben, "I might have told myself that, being a poor boy from the ghetto, I had too much to overcome to succeed in medical school. Why not reduce my load and forget about trying to do excellent work? But I decided not to take that route. I was intent on being a victor."

And that's what he became.

As Ben now says, "A victim walking through sand looks down and sees dirt; a victor sees the ingredients for building a castle."

Looking for shortcuts and doing no more than what's required just to "get by" seldom leads to victory.

FROM GOD'S WORD:

A lazy person will end up poor, but a hard worker will become rich (Proverbs 10:4, NCV).

LET'S TALK ABOUT IT:

1. Why didn't Ben do what his advisor suggested by going into some other field or taking his classes more slowly?
2. What hardships from Ben's past might he have used as excuses for not doing his best?
3. What does it mean to think of yourself as a victim? Why is that dangerous?

ELIZA DAVIS GEORGE

Liberia's American "Mother"

Eliza Davis was born in Texas on January 20, 1879, and died in Texas in 1979—one hundred years later. Living to be a hundred years old is a remarkable thing, but not nearly as remarkable as how Eliza spent those years.

For most African-Americans after the Civil War, life was a constant struggle. Poverty, lack of education, and continuing discrimination were the critical issues facing black leaders well into the twentieth century. But to Eliza Davis, American blacks had one source of wealth worth sharing: the Gospel of Jesus Christ. While studying for her teaching certificate, Eliza heard a pastor who had just returned from Liberia. "The people are lost in pagan religions because no one has taken the Gospel to them. Who will go? White missionaries, you say? These are *our* people! *Our* ancestors! *We* have a responsibility to share the Good News with our brothers and sisters in Africa."

The pastor's words burned deep in Eliza's heart. She finished college and taught school for several years, but "the call" grew stronger. She had to go to Africa.

Eliza Davis turned thirty-five the day the ship *Celtic* nosed into the docks of Monrovia on January 20, 1914. The coast of Liberia had several "civilized" cities of "Americo-Liberians"—former American slaves, or descendents of slaves, who had returned to their homeland—and many churches. But Eliza turned her heart to the native tribal people in the interior who had never heard of Jesus.

Her vision was to teach the children, whom she hoped would teach their own people. But in 1917, the National Baptist Association sent a married couple to replace her at the school she had established. What was she going to do now?

Eliza got a startling proposal from a black gentleman, a British citizen: "I'll help you start a new mission if you'll marry me." Eliza married G. Thompson George on January 12, 1918, and together they established the Kelton Mission. She became "Mother George" to hundreds of children, several of whom she adopted as her own and even brought to the United States for further education.

But money from Eliza's supporters arrived only sporadically. Several times Eliza and "Mr. George" traveled back to the United States to speak to churches and raise support. Often Mother George returned to Liberia, only to find the mission buildings destroyed by termites and the people scattered. She had to begin the work all over again.

Still, Eliza held on to her vision of training Liberians to teach Liberians. And finally all the seeds she had sown in the stubborn soil of Liberia took root. The Elizabeth Native Interior Mission (ENI) became the umbrella for many schools for tribal children, as well as a maternity clinic; the Eliza Davis George Pastor's Training School sent out hundreds of native church leaders to establish churches.

For her labor of love, Mother George was awarded a knighthood and a citation as "Grande Dame Commander" in the Republic of Liberia shortly before her death on March 8, 1979. "One hundred years old is old enough."

PERSEVERANCE
Two Hundred Miles by
Ankle-Express

other Eliza George finished the pile of mending and glanced at the noonday sun beating down on the wood and thatch buildings in the jungle clearing. It was time to call the children together for prayer.

Lifting her strong, clear voice, Mother George began to sing, "Jesus, Keep Me Near the Cross." All over Kelton Mission, children of all ages stopped what they were doing and ran toward the thin, brown-skinned American woman whom they called "Mother." As they clustered around her, she began to pray for each of the children by name. Then came prayers that Mr. George would come back to Liberia soon and that their supporters in America would send the money they so desperately needed to pay their debts and buy food, clothes, and schoolbooks for the children.

As the children settled down to their meager noon meal of rice and vegetables, a man appeared out of the jungle. "Mother," he called, "a steamer arrived yesterday in Greenville. Maybe . . ."

The words were hardly out of his mouth before Mother George jumped up, disappeared inside her thatched-roof house, and reappeared wearing her sun helmet and big rubber boots for walking the jungle trails. "Maude," she told her eighteen-year-old adopted daughter, "see that the children keep on with their lessons and chores. Robert and Tussnah, you come with me. We're going for the mail!"

Walking the twenty miles to Greenville was not unusual for Mother George. She often tramped from village to village by "ankle-express," as she laughingly called it, sharing the Gospel. Today she hardly noticed the miles as they slogged their way through the swampy jungle. Surely there would be money waiting for them.

When the trio finally arrived, Mother George marched directly to the post office. "Any mail for Mother?" The clerk handed her a batch of letters . . . yes! A letter from Mr. George. She ripped open the envelope but found only a letter. *One of the churches sent you $200. I hope you have received it.*

Had she missed something? But all she found was a notice from the post office in Monrovia: *"A postal order for $200 has been received for you. Please pick it up within thirty days."* Monrovia? The capital city was two hundred miles away! Frantically, Mother George looked at the date the notice had been sent. Four weeks ago! Was it too late?

"Robert . . . Tussnah, come. We have no time to lose. We're going to Monrovia."

The boys looked confused. "But, Mother, the steamer has already left. We have no way to get there."

"Oh yes, we do." Her eyes had a determined look. "Ankle-express." And so the trio set off along the beach, heading north. Each long, hot day blurred into the next. The cool seawater soothed their burning, blistered feet. Fishermen and villagers along the way gave them a meal or a grass mat for the night. They often had to wait for the tide to go out before they could get around a rocky point.

Finally, six days later, their feet swollen and bleeding, Mother George and the two boys dragged into Monrovia and made their way to the post office. Wearily, Mother handed the clerk the notice about the postal order. The clerk frowned. "I'm sorry, Mrs. George. No one came to claim it, so we sent it back to the United States last week."

Tussnah broke down with a loud wail. Mother George wiped away her own tears of disappointment. Should she give up now? No! Hadn't God brought her to Liberia? Her work wasn't finished yet. Somehow, sometime, some way, God would provide the money to keep the mission school going. But right now, all she could do was return home again the same way she had come—by ankle-express.

Perseverance often depends on how strongly
we believe in our goal.

FROM GOD'S WORD:
Love never gives up, never loses faith, is always hopeful, and endures through every circumstance (1 Corinthians 13:7).

LET'S TALK ABOUT IT:
1. What did you think was going to happen when Mother George finally got to Monrovia?
2. How do you usually react when something you want very much doesn't happen? (Give up? Get mad? Blame God?)
3. Discuss: Sometimes we say God is "shutting a door" when things don't happen the way we had hoped. Other times, God wants us to keep hold of our goal, even when bad things happen. How do we know the difference?

ENCOURAGEMENT
Snip and Stitch

am! Bam! The teenage boy pounded the last post into the ground with his big wooden mallet and stood back to look at the sturdy fence. *That* should keep the forest "critters" out of the mission garden.

"Good job, Charles Carpenter," came a woman's voice. Charles jumped. He hadn't heard Mother George come up behind him. The American missionary was grinning from ear to ear. "You are certainly living up to your name! You are a hard worker."

Embarrassed, Charles looked at his bare toes. He had lived in the forests of Liberia his whole life up till now and still wasn't used to his new name and the "civilized ways" here at Kelton Mission. But he liked this American woman whose skin was the same color as his own and who treated him no differently than the town boys who came to her school. But . . . there was something that bothered him.

"What is it, son?" she said, as if reading his mind.

He felt his ears burn. "I . . . my clothes . . ." He was ashamed of the tattered pants he'd been wearing ever since he arrived at the mission.

"Of course! You need a new pair of pants. Mercy me, why didn't I think of this before?"

The next day Charles scurried along the jungle trail toward Greenville with money in his pocket for a new pair of pants. He felt like a grown man walking into the tailor's shop to order his own pair of pants.

The tailor was busy with another customer. Charles waited and waited. The other customer left. Still Charles waited. Finally he cleared his throat. "I would like to order—"

"What? Get out! Shoo, shoo," said the tailor. "Don't want no country boys in my shop."

"But I have money—"

"Money? You probably stole it. Go on, now, get out." And the door slammed firmly behind him.

Humiliated, Charles walked the twenty miles back to Kelton Mission.

When he told Mother George what had happened, her eyes got a determined look. "Then you shall learn to sew yourself!" she announced.

The next day, Charles found himself on the trail back to Greenville with money in his pocket for room and food. He found a different tailor and asked if he could watch. For several weeks, he hung around the shop, watching the tailor measure and snip and sew. Then he went back to the mission and reported what he'd been learning.

Mother George gave him a piece of cloth and a pair of scissors and sent him back to Greenville. Now when the tailor measured, he measured; when he cut, Charles cut. Back at the mission he stitched up the pants. What a mess! The seams were bunched and crooked. But Mother George held them up and said, "You are learning so fast! I know that you will soon be sewing clothes for the whole mission!"

Back to Greenville. This time Charles watched and measured and cut even more carefully. This time the pants he sewed up were much better. Again and again he practiced. And the next time a bolt of cloth arrived at the mission, Mother George handed the whole bolt to

Charles and said casually, "The little boys need new pants."

Many years later, Charles married Lu, a mission girl whom Mother George had taken under her wing, and she sent out the young couple to establish another school for children in the forest. Looking back, Charles said, "I was an ignorant country boy, but Mother George believed in me. From that time on, I made a special effort to please her, because she believed I was just as important to God as the town boys."

An encourager sees people as God sees them—each person has value, with gifts and talents that need to be encouraged.

FROM GOD'S WORD:
So encourage each other and build each other up, just as you are already doing (1 Thessalonians 5:11).

LET'S TALK ABOUT IT:
1. What qualities in Charles did Mother George see that made her confident that he could learn to be a tailor?
2. In what ways did she encourage him? (Make a list!)
3. Is there someone you could encourage today? How?

SACRIFICE
"Son, Take It"

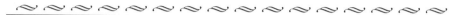

other Eliza Davis George proudly listened to Augustus Marwieh deliver the valedictory speech for the 1953 graduating class of the College of Liberia. Could this really be the same "country boy" who had come to her mission when he was only fifteen? Even though he was the son of a tribal chief, he couldn't read or write. Now look at him!

Ever since Mother George had come to Africa, she'd had a dream—that a young Liberian from the "uncivilized" tribes would be educated, trained, and then come back to be a missionary to his own people. Mother knew she was getting old. She needed someone who could take over her work.

She had taken several promising girls to America to be educated. But one got sick and died, one married an American, one liked "town life." But Gus . . . surely Gus was the one God had chosen to take over her work. As the old woman and young man walked the jungle trails to visit the villagers, she listened as he shared the great burden he had for his own people. Yes, yes, Gus was the one.

Mother George eagerly followed Gus's progress as he continued his schooling in America—first Simpson College, then Golden Gate

Seminary in San Francisco. When Mother had to return to the U.S. for an emergency eye operation, she thought, *I'll surprise Gus and go see him!*

But she wasn't prepared for the surprise he had for her. "Mother, this is Donna," Gus said, introducing a lovely American girl. "We are in love, and she has agreed to marry me and come to Africa with me to work in the mission."

Sadly, Mother George shook her head. "Oh, dear young people. This is not God's choice for you. Donna may think she shares your call to return to your people in the jungles of Liberia. But mission life is hard. One day you will be forced to choose between God's call and a wife who will be homesick and not used to the rigors of jungle life."

Gus felt heartbroken. But he respected Mother too much to ignore her advice. Sadly, he and Donna broke their engagement. Then, on Mother's advice, he chose a fine young woman from the ENI mission to be his bride—a girl named Othelia.

Mother George was still on furlough when Gus sailed back to Africa in 1960 to meet his bride and take up duties at the mission. But a letter from Gus soon found her in Texas. *"Dr. William Tolbert has asked me to be assistant principal of the Liberian Baptist school in Monrovia. They are desperate for qualified staff. What should I do, Mother?"*

As Mother George read the letter, she felt her hopes crumbling. Dr. William Tolbert was the vice president of Liberia, as well as president of the Liberian Baptist Association. Why did she think she could keep such a brilliant and well-educated young man as Augustus Marwieh for her own little mission out in the bush? But she was eighty-one years old. Who would take over the mission now?

Eliza Davis George fell to her knees in prayer and committed the ENI mission to God. Then she got off her knees and sent a telegram to Gus: *"Son, take it."*

Gus took the job. But he couldn't stop thinking about his people in the forests of Liberia. Five years later he resigned. What a joyous homecoming at the mission! Now Mother George could rest, knowing that her work would be in Gus's capable hands.

"What did Othelia say?" asked Mother George. She knew it wasn't easy to give up their nice house and car and good salary in Monrovia to return to the forest, where many villages still could only be reached by "ankle-express."

Gus grinned. "You picked a good wife for me, Mother. Othelia said, 'If God is leading us to go, let's go.'"

Sometimes we have to sacrifice our own plans
and trust God to work things out
in His own way and His own time.

FROM GOD'S WORD:
"Father . . . not my will, but yours be done" (Luke 22:42, NIV).

LET'S TALK ABOUT IT:
1. Why did Mother George think Gus Marwieh was the person God intended to take over the mission work when she got too old?
2. Why do you think Mother George advised Gus to take the job, even though she had to sacrifice her own hopes for him? How did God work it out?
3. Parents, share with your children a time when you had to "let go" of your own plans and trust God to work things out. What was the result?

JOHN HARPER

———— ⚜ ————

The *Titanic's* Last Hero

Born to a Scottish family on May 29, 1872, in the village of Houston in Renfrewshire, John Harper grew up surrounded by a solid Christian faith. As a lad, he faithfully attended church, was not rebellious or wild, and at the age of fourteen, gave his life to the Lord. But like many boys of his time, he was eager to prove his manhood by getting a job; while still in his teens he went to work in the local paper mill.

But in 1890, just after his eighteenth birthday, he was home alone on a fine June day and had what he called a vision from God. God showed him that "good" people and "wicked" people are both lost without Christ, and that Christ's death on the cross was the *only* thing that had saved him. He was overwhelmed by God's great love, and a passion began to grow within him to share God's love and win "the lost" for Christ. After a long workday in the paper mill, he would go to the surrounding villages and preach on the street corners.

In 1896 an English pastor from a Baptist mission in London heard about the young street-corner evangelist and invited him to become part of their mission in Govan, a "burgh" of Glasgow, Scotland. After a year and a half, he was sent to Gordon Halls on Paisley Road (near Glasgow) and started the Paisley Road Baptist Church with twenty-five members. A few years later, a church building was erected nearby out of corrugated iron, which came to be nicknamed "the Iron Church."

John Harper not only had the zeal of an evangelist, but a pastor's heart. Within thirteen years, Paisley Road Baptist Church had grown to five hundred people. But during this time he was severely tested. In 1904 he married Annie Bell, who brought great joy to his life, but that joy was short-lived. Two years later she gave birth to a daughter but died shortly afterward, leaving behind a motherless infant. A year earlier (1905), John had been seriously ill for six months, which left both his body and powerful voice weakened.

But John Harper's faith was in God, and he still wanted to share the Gospel. In September 1910, he left the thriving Paisley Road church to become pastor of the Walworth Road Baptist Church in London. News of his powerful preaching and the many people who were being saved under his ministry spread, and he was invited by Moody Church in Chicago to conduct "special services" in the winter of 1911–1912. The special services became a revival, and he was invited to return to Chicago in April 1912. Harper booked passage for himself and six-year-old Nana on the *Lusitania*, but for reasons unknown changed his ticket to the *Titanic*, which sailed from London on April 10.

John Harper never arrived in Chicago. Little Nana was saved when the "unsinkable ship" sank five nights later, but John Harper went down with the ship. His actions that fateful night can only be described as heroic. He was thirty-nine years old, still a young man, but in both heavenly and earthly terms, he can well be called "the *Titanic*'s last hero."

ZEAL
Crowning King Jesus

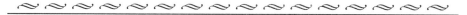

aul Morris[2] put on his cap, stuck the day's newspaper under his arm, and walked jauntily to his girl's house on the outskirts of Glasgow, Scotland. "Would've been grand to be in London today." He grinned as the young couple settled on a bench in her mother's garden. Paul opened up the paper and jabbed a thick finger at the headlines under the date—August 9, 1902. "Just imagine all that pomp and ceremony when they crowned King Edward!"

"Aye, that'd sure be a sight," murmured Glynis, but she seemed distracted. "Don'na know what to do about tomorrow, though."

"Tomorrow?" said her suitor absently, his mind still on the king's coronation.

Glynis sighed. "Some church workers came by the house last night—they got a promise from Mama that we'd come to the church services over on Paisley Road tomorrow night."

Paul snorted. "Is that the church that's been holding outdoor services all summer? Lots of preachin' and hallelujahs and loud amens?"

Glynis giggled. "That's the one. Come with me. Just for a lark."

---

[2]Note: We do not know this person's name, only his initials: P. C. M.

"Humph. Can think of a lot of things I'd rather do with my Sunday evening," he mumbled.

But Sunday evening, August 10, found a reluctant Paul escorting his girl into the Paisley Road Baptist Church. Two deacons shook their hands warmly and showed them to a seat. As the service began, an open hymnbook was put into their hands. The singing was hearty—a definite improvement, Paul thought, over the sleepy drone that passed for hymn singing at his own church. But then a tall, slender man—John Harper, the pastor of Paisley Road Baptist Church—announced the sermon text: Isaiah 44:20. The pastor's voice was powerful as he read the Scripture: " 'He feedeth on ashes. . . .' "

Paul Morris couldn't remember exactly what the pastor said—only that John Harper's words cut like a knife into his soul. Paul realized that "religion" by itself was like eating ashes. Going to church couldn't save him. Only Jesus Christ could do that. At the end of the service, Pastor Harper asked all those who wanted to trust Christ as Savior to raise their hand. Paul Morris's hand shot up. And in that moment he realized an important transfer had taken place: He got off the throne of his life and crowned Jesus king.

After church, one of the members stopped to talk to Paul and his sweetheart. "Are you trusting Jesus?" the man asked Glynis.

She shrugged but replied honestly, "No."

"What about you, young man?"

Paul squared his shoulders. "Yes."

Glynis's eyes widened. "That's not true!" she cried. "You didn't even want to come tonight."

But the church member persisted. "How long have you known Christ as Savior?"

"Since Pastor Harper gave the invitation just a few minutes ago." Turning to Glynis, Paul said, "It's true, I didn't want to come. But Pastor Harper's sermon convinced me that I need Jesus. I asked Him to come into my life and save me."

To Paul's surprise, Glynis began to weep, and within a few minutes she, too, asked Jesus to be her Savior.

As the young couple, soon to be married, walked away from Paisley Road Baptist Church, they passed an old man and heard the church member ask him, "Are you trusting in Jesus?"

"Oh yes," said the old man. "Nine years now."

"How old were you then?"

"Just turned seventy."

"And how did it come about?"

Curious, Paul and Glynis turned to hear the last bit of conversation with the old man. White-haired and bent, he still had a wide smile. "Nine years ago there was no church here. But that young man—that Mr. Harper—he was out on a street corner preaching Jesus, and I trusted Him as Savior there and then."

Zeal is doing something for God
with everything you've got.

FROM GOD'S WORD:
Love the Lord your God with all your heart, all your soul, all your mind, and all your strength (Mark 12:30).

LET'S TALK ABOUT IT:
1. From this story, what do you think Pastor John Harper wanted to do more than anything?
2. How do you know he was willing to give it "everything he got"?
3. What are some ways you can love God with *all* your heart? *All* your soul? *All* your mind? *All* your strength?

INTERCESSION
"Dear John Is Far Ben"

George Harper paid the horse-and-carriage cab driver and entered the door of the "Iron Kirk"—the nickname given to the Paisley Road Baptist Church, which had been built of corrugated iron. Almost immediately his brother swept him into a bear hug.

"George!" cried John Harper, pastor of the rapidly growing church. "I'm so glad you've come. Are you ready to preach?"

George didn't answer. Instead, he looked his brother over with a critical but loving eye. He knew that the last few years had been difficult for John. First there had been the six-month illness that had drained energy from his tall, slender body and weakened the powerful preaching voice. Then there was the birth of his baby daughter, Nana—which should have been a joyous time, except that John's wife, Annie, did not recover from the birth of the child and slipped away into eternity.

"How's little Nana?" he asked gently. George and his wife had cared for the motherless infant for six months and would have willingly raised her, but John was desperate to hold on to some form of family life and took little Nana back home to live with him.

John smiled. "She's fine, fine. Growing like a weed. Are you ready to preach tonight?"

George laughed and gave in. "Yes, John—for you, I will preach."

As the evening service began at Paisley Road Baptist Church, George saw his brother leave the platform and slip into a small room at the side. He did not return for the entire service. When the preaching was over, the invitation given, and the last hymn sung, George shook a few hands, made his way to the small room, and opened the door a crack. John was on his knees, praying aloud for his brother George's sermon that night, praying for the service, praying that souls would be saved. He didn't even know that the service had ended.

A deacon came alongside George and peeked through the door that George had opened slightly. "Is he all right?" the man whispered with concern.

George nodded. "Dear John is far ben," he said quietly. The deacon smiled with understanding. "Ben" meant the innermost private part of a house in nineteenth century Scotland. Pastor John was deep in prayer.

The deacons locked up after the last person had left, but still a light burned in the little room. After a while, John Harper came out and began to walk up and down the rows of chairs in the empty sanctuary, praying first for this church member who sat here and then that family who sat there. Far into the wee hours of the night, he continued to pray by name for the people of his church.

The next morning George expressed his concern. "John, you still have not regained your strength from your illness. You need more rest. You can't pray all night like this."

John just smiled and gathered his young daughter into his arms. "On the contrary, George. We need to pray more, not less." Nana wiggled out of her father's arms and ran off to play. "Now, George," John said, "I need some brotherly advice. Moody Bible Institute in Chicago has asked me to come preach for three months of special services this coming winter. What do you think? Should I go? Should I take Nana with me?"

George shook his head at his stubborn, single-minded brother and grinned. "Let's pray about it."

Intercession is praying constantly for others,
not for our own wants and needs.

FROM GOD'S WORD:
Keep on praying (1 Thessalonians 5:17).

LET'S TALK ABOUT IT:
1. Why do you think John Harper decided to pray during the service instead of listening to his brother preach?
2. Does your family tend to sit in the same place in church each Sunday? If you attended John Harper's church, how would you feel if you discovered that he walked around the empty church, stopped by the place your family usually sat, and prayed for you and your family?
3. What does it mean to you to "keep on praying," "pray continually" (NIV), or "pray without ceasing" (KJV)?

SELF-SACRIFICE
"It Will Be Beautiful in the Morning"

≈≈≈≈≈≈≈≈≈≈≈≈≈≈≈≈≈≈≈≈≈≈

ohn Harper held little Nana's hand tightly as they walked the deck of the big ship. He smiled at the child fondly, thinking how much she looked like the mother she had never known.

"Papa, this ship is so *big*!" Nana said as they rounded the bow and started back down the other side of the *Titanic*. "It's as big as a whole city!"

John chuckled and was about to agree, when he noticed a young man hunched beside the deck rail. "Just a minute, darling . . . this young man looks like he needs to hear the Good News."

Nana peeked through the rails and patiently watched the sun settling down on the edge of the water as she listened to the familiar sound of her father explaining how to be saved. After a while the young man turned and walked away. Nana once again put her hand in her father's and pointed at the horizon. "Look, Papa—the sky is so red!"

"Yes, I see, darling. 'Red sky at night, sailors delight . . .' It's going to be beautiful in the morning."

It was late. Nana should be in bed. John Harper took his little girl and tucked her into her bunk in their cabin, then settled down at the tiny desk to read by lamplight before going to bed himself.

Shortly before midnight the ship seemed to shudder. Not long afterward, urgent voices were heard in the narrow hallway. "Everybody out! Everybody out!" John pulled on his clothes, bundled Nana into her cloak, and went up on deck. Panic spread the word: An iceberg had grazed the ship, tearing open a gaping hole, and the ship was taking on water.

Life jackets were handed out. People started pushing and scrambling to get into the lifeboats. "Let the women, children, and the unsaved into the lifeboats!" John shouted. He swung little Nana into a lifeboat, then turned back to help others as flares shot into the sky.

John spotted a man without a life jacket. "Are you saved, brother?" he asked. The man looked at him angrily and tried to brush him aside. "Here," said John, taking off his life jacket. "You need this more than I do."

As the dark, cold waters of the North Atlantic crept up the decks of the *Titanic*, John Harper's calm, reasoning voice could be heard helping to load people into the lifeboats, and asking first one, then another and another, "Brother . . . sister, are you saved? It's not too late! Ask God to forgive your sins and accept Jesus as your Lord and Savior. Be sure where you will spend eternity!"

At 2:20 A.M., the stern of the giant ship rose in the air, and the *Titanic* began its long plunge to the bottom of the ocean. John Harper was thrown into the icy water. All around him were the desperate cries of drowning men and women. A man clinging to a board drifted near the floundering Harper. "Are you saved?" Harper shouted.

"No," the man gasped.

"Believe on the Lord Jesus Christ, and thou shall be saved," John Harper shouted back.

The icy waters were taking their toll. John Harper's strength was giving out. He saw the man float back within calling distance. "Are you saved?" he shouted again.

"No," came the weak reply.

"Then believe on the Lord Jesus Christ, and thou shall be saved," he urged before slipping beneath the water.

The man clinging to the board was later picked up by a rescue ship. John Harper's last words burned in his mind, and he gave his heart to Christ. He was John Harper's last convert.

As the sun rose on the scene of the disaster on April 15, 1912, it *was* a beautiful morning—but for John Harper, that morning was in heaven, where he met the Savior he loved so much, face-to-face.

Self-sacrifice is loving as Jesus loved—a willingness to give up my life so that others might live.

FROM GOD'S WORD:

This is my command: Love each other as I have loved you. The greatest love a person can show is to die for his friends (John 15:12–13, NCV).

LET'S TALK ABOUT IT:

1. Why do you think John Harper didn't get into the lifeboat with Nana, even though he knew she would become an orphan?
2. Everybody on the *Titanic* wanted to be "saved" from drowning. But when John Harper asked, "Are you saved?" what did he mean?
3. Are *you* saved?

SAMUEL LEIGH

———— ❧ ————

Pioneer Missionary to Australia

Few places were as wild and woolly as New South Wales, Australia, in 1815 when Samuel Leigh arrived as the first Methodist missionary.

Samuel had been born near Hanley, Staffordshire, England, on September 1, 1785. When he was only three years old the first European settlement in Australia was established by England. The government had decided that the best way to get rid of its growing prison population and other "undesirables" was to send them all to the opposite side of the world and let them fight it out among themselves. (See the TRAILBLAZER BOOK *The Thieves of Tyburn Square*.)

Some of those "transported" to Australia were hardened criminals. Others were guilty of little more than stealing a loaf of bread when they were hungry. The rough life created by this mix of about twenty thousand people in the colonial towns of New South Wales had little moral restraint. Crime, drunkenness, and adultery were common. But desperation sometimes leads people to reach out to God. In 1814 a committee of twelve Australian "citizens" wrote to the Methodist Missionary Society in London, begging them to *"send us that gospel which you have received from the Lord to preach to every creature."*

By then Samuel Leigh had been trained as a missionary by the Society and was prepared to go to Montreal. But with Canada still embroiled in the War of 1812 with the United States, that assignment did not seem wise. So the Society sent Samuel to Australia.

Leigh began services in Sydney in a rented house where the partitions had been removed so that he could have a "preaching room" for the congregation, but he soon moved out from Sydney to bring the Gospel to the settlers scattered throughout the countryside. Similar to Peter Cartwright (see *Hero Tales II*) and other circuit-riding preachers on the American frontier, Leigh developed a 150-mile circuit that he traveled every ten days on horseback, stopping at fifteen preaching places. This meant traveling in all kinds of weather, going without proper food, and often sleeping on the ground.

John Lees, a former soldier, was so grateful for Leigh's coming to preach the Gospel that he donated some of his land at Castlereagh and helped build the first Methodist chapel in Australia. Another soldier, Sergeant James, built at his own expense the first chapel in Sydney in his garden in Princes Street.

After establishing several churches in Australia and recruiting a few lay assistants, Samuel made several trips to New Zealand to serve the colony of settlers there as well as evangelize the headhunting cannibals of that land.

He believed that effective Christian witness required men "full of faith and of the Holy Ghost" who would not spare their own bodies. With only one year off (1820) to return to England, where he got married, Leigh drove himself in ministry in Australia and New Zealand until 1831, when his health totally broke down. He was forced to return to England, where he worked at more limited tasks until 1845. He finally died of the results of an earlier stroke on May 2, 1852, at the age of sixty-six.

RESISTING TEMPTATION
A Change of Plans?

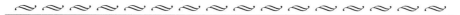

hen Samuel Leigh got off the ship in Sydney, his welcome was not as warm as his invitation to come to Australia had been. "I'm sorry to inform you," said his host, Edward Eager, "that it is now doubtful whether the governor will allow you to remain in the country as a missionary."

In shock, Samuel went the next day to speak to the governor.

"Who sent you here as a missionary?" asked Governor Lachlan Macquarie.

"The Methodist Missionary Society," said Samuel, "at the request of several of your British subjects here in Australia. And," he quickly added, "I'm here with the approval of His Majesty's government."

The governor frowned and shook his head slowly. "Well, it's too bad you came here as a missionary, because I can't give you any encouragement in that regard—"

"But I have documents," interrupted Samuel, forgetting his manners and pulling out his papers. "They show that I am legally and duly authorized to preach the Gospel in any part of His Majesty's kingdom."

The governor impatiently waved his hand across his face, as though shooing away a fly. "Those documents are of no value here." He shook his finger in Samuel's face. "Young man, you have come to a strange and harsh country, and the sooner you realize that, the better." He paused, then his tone softened. "However, we do need some help here in the government—such as it is. You seem like a bright young man. I can find you a job, which could lead to a very powerful position."

"But . . . but I was sent here to preach the Gospel."

"Look, if it's money you want, I can get you a good position as a schoolmaster. You will be far more comfortable than going around preaching to the likes of the riffraff around here. Just change your plans a little."

Samuel swallowed. He didn't want to be rude. Did he really know what he was in for? But he didn't flinch. "Thank you, Governor, but I cannot accept your offer. I was sent to this country as a missionary, and I cannot act in any other capacity while I remain here."

Before the governor could protest, Samuel explained his goals of winning people to Christ and starting small churches to teach and encourage new believers. He was certain Christian converts would be far better citizens than the angry and resentful criminals that currently made up the population of New South Wales.

The governor scratched his chin thoughtfully. "Hmm. If those are your objectives, you might end up making life easier for me. This is a tough lot to govern." He shrugged and turned his palms up in a helpless gesture. "What can I say? I wish you all the success you can reasonably expect or desire. You have my blessing, and I will instruct my officials to assist you in every way possible."

Samuel gave a polite bow of gratitude and turned to go. He had resisted the temptation to take the easy way out. But he knew there would be lots of temptations ahead.

*Even Jesus had to resist the temptation
to take the "easier" way.*

FROM GOD'S WORD:
Be strong and very courageous. Obey all the laws Moses
gave you. Do not turn away from them, and you will be
successful in everything you do (Joshua 1:7).

LET'S TALK ABOUT IT:
1. How do you think Samuel felt when Edward Eager told
   him things weren't working out as planned when he
   arrived in Australia?
2. Why do you think the governor's job offers might have
   tempted Samuel?
3. Read the story of Jesus' temptation in Matthew 4:1–11.
   What might have happened if Jesus had taken the
   "easier" way?

OBEDIENCE
Going the Extra
Two Miles

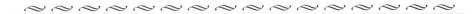

 nce church services got started in Sydney, Samuel Leigh bought a horse to take the Gospel to settlers in the surrounding countryside. But where would he start?

"Could you visit a friend of mine in Castlereagh?" asked one of the new Christians in Sydney. "I'll give you a letter of introduction."

Early one morning, Samuel set out on the thirty-five-mile trip through the thick woods. He arrived exhausted just after the sun had set and called out to the man who was standing on his porch, "Sir, I have a letter from your friend in Sydney. He hopes you will allow me as a missionary to preach to you and your household."

The man scowled. "I will not allow it." His arms were crossed, his head back.

Samuel's shoulders dropped. Why had he come all the way out here alone in this wilderness, anyway? "Then would you allow me to pasture my horse and sleep in your barn for the night? I'll pay you whatever it's worth to you."

"I will not allow it."

Samuel looked around him. Why had God led him all the way out here in the middle of nowhere to be treated so rudely? Finally he said, "Can you think of *anyone* in these parts who might take me in for the night?"

"John Lees might. Lives a couple miles over that direction." The settler jerked his head, refusing to uncross his arms even to give better directions.

Samuel nearly turned for home, but instead he urged his tired horse and rode on through the tangled brush, hoping to find the homestead of John Lees before it got too dark to travel. When he arrived at Lees' wood hut, he was so tired that he did not even get off his horse but tapped on the door with his riding whip. "Is there anyone here who would receive a tired missionary?"

The door flung open, and out came a sturdy boy who grabbed the horse's bridle. "Get off, sir! My father will gladly see you."

Samuel dropped down stiffly and entered the hut. Around a table sat several people leaning over some open Bibles.

"Praise God!" said Mr. Lees. "We were just going to have family worship. We've been praying for three years that God would send us a missionary. Here, sir, take this chair. Perhaps you would read to us."

Samuel sat down and found the place indicated in Isaiah 35. " 'The wilderness and the solitary place shall be glad for them; and the desert shall rejoice, and blossom as the rose' " (KJV). Tears began rolling down Samuel's cheeks. He could not be in a more remote wilderness, and yet here he was gladly received.

Five minutes earlier he had felt like a stranger in a strange land, alone in the woods with no place to stay while the night closed in. But now he was among new friends who were rejoicing that he had come.

Samuel discovered that Mr. Lees had been a terrible drunk who had nearly ruined his family by selling everything they had to get alcohol. He was ready to sell their last valuable possession—a pig ready for market—when he had a terrible nightmare in which a deadly snake rose out of his liquor bottle, attempting to strike him.

This dream so frightened him that he called out to God and began to read the Bible, totally changing his life. But there was no one to teach him or his family more about being a Christian . . . until Samuel Leigh came riding through the night.

John Lees was so grateful that he donated some of his land and began building a chapel so there would be a place for other homesteaders to meet whenever Samuel Leigh came their way again. After that, Samuel rode his circuit about every ten days.

We may not understand what God has planned until after we obey.

FROM GOD'S WORD:
I will instruct you and teach you in the way you should go; I will counsel you and watch over you (Psalm 32:8, NIV).

LET'S TALK ABOUT IT:
1. Why did Samuel make a hard thirty-five-mile trip into the wilderness in the first place?
2. What might have happened if he had not gone on the extra two miles?
3. As a family, talk about times when you obeyed God by doing the "right" thing even though you didn't feel like it. What was the result?

RESOURCEFULNESS
The Fishhook Escape

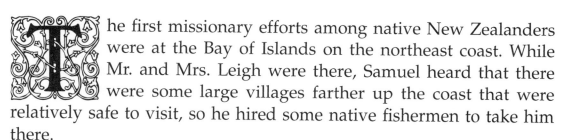

The first missionary efforts among native New Zealanders were at the Bay of Islands on the northeast coast. While Mr. and Mrs. Leigh were there, Samuel heard that there were some large villages farther up the coast that were relatively safe to visit, so he hired some native fishermen to take him there.

But a storm came up suddenly and drove them out to sea. Night had fallen before the storm subsided, and the moon came out. Fortunately, they could still see land and made their way toward it. But the waves were so high along the coast that they had to enter Wangaroa Bay. Around its shores lived some of the fiercest cannibals on the island. Several years earlier when the ship *Boyd* had stopped there, they had killed and eaten nearly seventy crew members and passengers. Except for a well-armed party that rescued five survivors, Samuel was the first white man to venture back into that bay.

When they landed, the natives gathered around in a hostile manner, but Samuel convinced the chief that they were there only because of the storm and would leave the next morning. The chief agreed and put Samuel and his sailors in a hut. Being so exhausted, Samuel fell right asleep, thankful that God had protected them.

Just before daybreak, his men awoke him in alarm. "Listen," they whispered. "They are arguing over the best time tomorrow to roast and eat us."

"Don't worry," said Samuel. "They can't touch us without God's permission, and I am sure He has not yet consented to our being either killed or eaten. Go back to sleep."

Samuel then slept until 8:00, when he rose and went outside. Every action of the natives seemed to indicate that they were preparing for a huge feast—of their guests—and would probably attack as soon as the visitors made an attempt to leave. Samuel was just as eager to leave the place as his crew, but he knew that any sign of fear or haste would invite instant death. So he calmly went outside, and in front of 150 agitated natives, had breakfast, read his Bible, and then prayed.

"Chief Te Arā," he said, "would you take us for a little tour in our boat around your bay? I would like to see more of this beautiful place." (Chief Te Arā had actually visited Sydney for several months and could speak a little English.)

The chief readily agreed, and together they sailed north. "See that old burned-out ship hull?" said the chief. "That was the ship *Boyd*. Captain Thomas and his men were very rude and cruel to us. We killed and ate them."

When Samuel and his sailors returned to the beach, where the fierce natives were waiting, he walked with the chief into the middle of them, leaving his sailors with the canoe. As soon as they were far enough away from the canoe, Samuel stopped. The chief drifted away, obviously unwilling to interfere. Samuel knew this was the moment. The natives were yelling and shaking their spears. Then the Holy Spirit gave him an idea.

Suddenly he pulled from his jacket pocket a large handful of tangled wires and held them up, shouting, "Stand back! I have fishhooks,

fishhooks, fishhooks!" As soon as he was sure that the men realized he did indeed have valuable hooks, Samuel threw them over their heads. The natives dove for them, pushing and shoving one another to find them in the sand.

Samuel turned and ran to catch the canoe his men had pushed safely out into the bay.

Though Samuel knew his life had been in great danger that day, he later returned when he knew the language better and established a mission among the tribespeople. Many responded by accepting Christ, and the entire tribe abandoned cannibalism.

The best "resource" is the Holy Spirit.

FROM GOD'S WORD:
And when you are brought to trial . . . don't worry about what to say in your defense, for the Holy Spirit will teach you what needs to be said even as you are standing there (Luke 12:11–12).

LET'S TALK ABOUT IT:
1. Why did Samuel say "Don't worry" when he learned that the cannibals were talking about eating him and his men?
2. Whose idea was it to throw the fishhooks in the air to distract the cannibals?
3. Read and discuss how Paul escaped death in Acts 23:11–24.

C. S. LEWIS

The Writer Behind the Wardrobe

"Little Lea," the brown-shingled boyhood home of Clive Staples Lewis, was full of rambling rooms, cubbyholes, and books—all kinds of books for "Jack" (he hated the name Clive) and his older brother, Warren, to read. Together the brothers often created stories and imaginary places such as "Animal Land" and the "Boxon Nation."

Born on November 29, 1898, in Belfast, Ireland, in the nominal Christian home of Albert and Flora Lewis, Jack was only nine years old when his mother died of cancer. Unable to cope with the loss of his wife *and* the care of two growing boys, Albert Lewis sent Jack off with his brother to a series of boarding schools in England—Wynyard, Cherbourg, and Malvern College. Boarding schools could be hard on bookish boys who weren't very athletic. With Warren always three years ahead, Jack often suffered the bullying and abuse alone. He begged his father to let him come home, but his pleas fell on deaf ears.

Cherbourg was a pleasant exception. Jack made friends, admired his teachers, and chucked his vague Christian beliefs along the way.

Finally, when he was fifteen, he was allowed to tutor privately with an old teacher of his father's, W. T. Kirkpatrick. In this "home-school" environment, Jack's academic brilliance was unleashed, and he gained a scholarship to University College, Oxford, England.

World War I took both brothers to the battlefield in France. Jack was wounded, recovered, returned to duty, then was discharged just after his twentieth birthday. He resumed his studies at Oxford, living with the mother of an army buddy who had been killed in France. In 1925, at the age of twenty-seven, Lewis was elected a Fellow of Magdalen College, Oxford, where he taught English language and literature for the next twenty-nine years.

Even though C. S. Lewis considered himself an agnostic, he kept running into writers and thinkers like J. R. R. Tolkien and George MacDonald—people he admired—who still believed in God. How foolish! Yet he knew that the darkness within his spirit was gradually being exchanged for lightness and joy. In his autobiography, *Surprised by Joy*, Lewis wrote: *"When [my brother and I] set out [by motorcycle to the Shipsnade Zoo on September 28, 1931,] I did not believe that Jesus Christ was the Son of God, and when we reached the zoo, I did."*

Jack gathered a group of friends—Christian writers and thinkers—who became known as "The Inklings" and met together twice a week for sixteen years to stimulate and encourage one another. During this time, C. S. Lewis wrote prolifically in three areas: scholastic (e.g., *The Allegory of Love*); fiction (e.g., the NARNIA series for children; the SPACE TRILOGY for adults; *The Screwtape Letters; Till We Have Faces*); and Christian apologetics (e.g., *The Pilgrim's Regress; Mere Christianity; The Four Loves*), plus numerous essays.

In 1956 C. S. Lewis married Joy Davidman, an American with whom he had enjoyed a match of wits and a shared Christian faith. Jack and Joy had only four short years together at the Lewis home, "The Kilns," in Oxford, before she died in 1960 of cancer. Jack himself died three years later, just a week short of his sixty-fifth birthday, on November 22, 1963—the same day President Jack Kennedy was assassinated in the United States.

FRIENDSHIP
The Boy Next Door

Laughing and pushing, fifteen-year-old "Jack" Lewis and his brother, Warren, practically fell through the doorway of "Little Lea," the family home on the outskirts of Belfast, Ireland. Jack wanted to hug the house. Christmas break! Four whole weeks of refuge from the constant harassment from the upperclassmen back at Malvern College. ("Pick up my books, Lewis." "Polish my shoes, Lewis." "What's the matter, Lewis, can't you run? Big lout like you?") How had Warren put up with it when *he* went to Malvern?

No matter. They were home now, and it would be like old times—he and Warren going for rambles in the meadows, making up new "chapters" for the mythical land of "Boxon" they'd created as boys. Or hiding away in one of the upper rooms, surrounded by books and drawing pads, comfortable in their silence.

Eighteen-year-old Warren was looking through the mail. "I say, a letter from one of my old chums at Malvern! He's inviting me to a Christmas party in Belfast next weekend . . . and here's another, visiting his sister for the holidays."

"Let me see those letters." Albert Lewis, the boys' father, held out his hand. Jack could see sudden anger smoldering in his brother's eyes as their father read through Warren's letters. "You've just come home, Warren. I've got tickets to the theater. And Cousin Mary will be inviting us over. Don't think you'll have much time for gadding about with your chums." Albert Lewis marched into his study.

Jack's spirit sank. Was Warren going to be running off with his friends? Would his father and Cousin Mary talk endlessly about politics? His cozy holiday fantasy seemed to crumble into ashes, like a piece of paper thrown on the fire.

"I *won't* have Father reading my letters!" hissed Warren. "Look, Jack, keep an eye out for the postman and get any letters for me before Father sees them, all right? Oh, here's a note from Arthur, asking us to come over when we get home." A mocking smile cracked Warren's face as he tossed the note at Jack. "Never gives up, does he, little brother?"

Jack watched Warren swagger out the door. He looked at the note and sighed. Arthur Greeves was their next-door neighbor, about Warren's age. He'd been sickly as a child and never went out much. Without fail, Arthur always invited the Lewis boys to come over when they came home for the holidays, and without fail, Jack and Warren always found an excuse not to go. Surely sitting with Arthur would be *boring*.

But today Jack shrugged. Why not? Warren obviously had plans that didn't include him. And he didn't want to get caught talking "grown-up talk" with Father.

Mrs. Greeves seemed surprised to see Jack. "Arthur! Arthur! Look who's here! It's the young Lewis boy." She beamed as she showed Jack upstairs to Arthur's room.

Arthur was sitting on his bed, surrounded by books. Jack glanced at the title of a book on Arthur's desk: *Myths of the Norsemen*. His eyes widened. "Do *you* like that?"

Within minutes the next-door neighbors discovered they both loved Norse legends, Celtic myths, and Greek literature. Day after day found Jack at Arthur's house, listening to the opera Arthur was composing or sharing their favorite books. "What? You've never read the Brontë sisters? Or Sir Walter Scott?" cried Arthur. Jack shared his love for the bigness of nature—stars, seas, and mountains. Arthur taught Jack how to look for beauty in small things—a bird's nest, a flowering thistle, the unique pattern of a tiny snowflake.

Many years later, C. S. Lewis called Arthur Greeves, "after my brother, my oldest and most intimate friend."

Sometimes friendship is sitting right under our nose.

FROM GOD'S WORD:
Better is a neighbor nearby than a brother far away (Proverbs 27:10c, NKJV).

LET'S TALK ABOUT IT:
1. Why do you think things were "different" this time between Warren and Jack when they came home for the Christmas holiday?
2. Why do you think the Lewis brothers always made excuses so they wouldn't have to go to Arthur Greeves' house?
3. Is there someone who would like to be your friend that you haven't yet given a chance? What might happen if you tried?

LOYALTY
A Battlefield Promise

At last! C. S. "Jack" Lewis had finally passed his college entrance exams and gained admission to Oxford University—but it wasn't turning out quite like he had expected. World War I was sucking all of Britain's young men into the war, and the campus was almost empty. Part of the university was being used as a military hospital.

Jack enlisted in the University Officer Training Corps (UOTC), and rigid army training began right on Oxford's campus. Marching, rifle practice, sparse meals, camping in the rain, drills, drills, drills. The only bright spot was Jack's roommate—"Paddy" Moore from Bristol, England. The two eighteen-year-olds hit it off, and Paddy invited Jack to come home with him on their weekend leaves. Mrs. Moore and Paddy's sister Maureen provided pleasant conversation and homey comforts—something Jack had missed since his own mother died when he was only nine.

When officer training finished, Jack and Paddy got their orders: They were being sent to France. "Jack," said Paddy as they packed their gear, "what's going to happen to my mother if . . . if I don't come back?"

Jack didn't want to think about not coming back. But Paddy insisted. "Will you . . . will you take care of her and Maureen if I don't make it?"

Jack gripped Paddy's hand. "You have my promise."

Twice Jack Lewis ended up in a military hospital—once with "trench fever" and the second time after being wounded by shrapnel from an exploding shell. While recovering from his wounds, he heard that Paddy Moore was missing. Later Jack was transferred to a hospital back in Bristol, England, as a "stretcher case." Mrs. Moore came to visit him, still believing her son was alive. But then she got the dreaded telegram: Her son, Paddy Moore, had been killed in battle. A few weeks later, on November 11, 1918, the war was over.

Jack was in shock. Not once did he imagine he would have to carry out his promise. He wasn't even twenty years old yet!

But Mrs. Janey Moore and Jack Lewis bonded like mother and son. She and Maureen moved to Oxford so they could be close to her "adopted son." As he settled back into his studies, most days he went to their apartment for lunch and often spent the weekend there. During summer holidays he visited his father at Little Lea in Belfast but also spent many weeks of the holidays with Mrs. Moore and Maureen.

Soon Jack's brother, Warren, and other friends began to notice that Mrs. Moore was getting more and more demanding. She saved up chores for Jack to do when he visited; she got angry if he didn't come on the weekend. Even when he became a university professor, she insisted he come for lunch each day. Jack never complained.

When Albert Lewis died, Jack used his share of the money from the sale of Little Lea to purchase a country home near Oxford for himself, Mrs. Moore, and Maureen. Warren visited "The Kilns" regularly, and after he retired from the army, he, too, moved into the country house. But he was angry at the way Mrs. Moore treated Jack—bossing him around, fussing and complaining. How did his brother stand it?

But a promise was a promise, and Jack was a man of his word.

The Oxford teacher and popular writer continued to care for his army buddy's mother up until the day she died in 1951—the same year that *Prince Caspian*, the second in the popular Narnia allegories for children, was published.

Loyalty keeps a promise, even when it's hard.

FROM GOD'S WORD:
The Lord hates those who don't keep their word, but he delights in those who do (Proverbs 12:22).

LET'S TALK ABOUT IT:
1. Why do you think C. S. Lewis didn't think he'd ever have to actually "make good" on the promise he made to Paddy?
2. Why do you think he faithfully kept his promise, even though no one knew about it to begin with besides Paddy—and Paddy was dead?
3. Have you ever made a promise you didn't keep? If so, what can you do about it now to "keep your word"? (Parents, this is for you, too!)

IMAGINATION

How Narnia Came to Be

~~~~~~~~~~~~~~~~~~~~~~~~~~~~~~~~~

"Uncle Jack?" The little girl peeked into C. S. Lewis's study, where the university professor was reading. "What's behind the old wardrobe upstairs?"

Jack Lewis hid a smile. The little girl was one of many children who had been sent away from London to stay in homes in the countryside during World War II because of the threat of bombing. He had given the children staying at "The Kilns" the run of his rambling house outside Oxford, England. After all, he knew the delight of exploring empty rooms and musty wardrobes. As a child, he and his brother had sat inside his grandfather's wardrobe full of old coats and told stories to each other about a magical place called "Animal Land."

Lewis winked at the little girl. "I don't know," he teased. "Maybe there's a magical land on the other side. But if you get lost in there, be sure to come back—or what in the world would I tell your mother?"

As the little girl ran off to play, Lewis laid down his book and stared thoughtfully into the fireplace. Then he jotted a few notes: "Little girl . . . a wardrobe . . . a magical land on the other side . . ."

Other ideas crowded C. S. Lewis's active mind: a picture of a faun carrying an umbrella and several packages in a snowy wood . . . the heroic mouse that had been a main character in the "Animal Land" stories he'd made up as a boy . . . a picture of an evil witch riding a sleigh . . . a picture he'd seen of a magnificent golden lion . . .

Ten years later, C. S. Lewis published a children's book about four children—Peter, Susan, Edmund, and Lucy Pevensie—who were staying with a professor during the bombing of London, and they discovered a wardrobe that led into a magical land called Narnia, where they met a Faun, and the White Witch, and a lion named Aslan, the king of Narnia.

The book was called *The Lion, the Witch, and the Wardrobe*, which became the first in a series of books about the Land of Narnia. In the past fifty years, the Narnia series has sold over one hundred million copies and delighted children and adults all over the world.

The Narnia books, which grew out of C. S. Lewis's imagination, can be read as an adventure story, as a tale of magic and talking animals, and as an "allegory" of the story of Jesus. An allegory is similar to a parable—though usually longer. Jesus told "parables" or stories to help people understand a truth He was trying to teach them.

In 1954 a group of schoolchildren from Maryland wrote C. S. Lewis and asked why he wrote the story of Jesus as an allegory. Lewis wrote back: *"I said, 'Let us suppose that there was a land like Narnia and that [Jesus], as he became a Man in our world, [what if] he became a Lion there, and then imagine what would happen."*

When C. S. Lewis wrote *The Lion, the Witch, and the Wardrobe*, he hadn't planned on writing another book about Narnia. But his imagination kept tossing ideas around. What if the Pevensie children returned to Narnia (*Prince Caspian*)? What about a heroic mouse that became the most valiant talking animal (Reepicheep in *Prince Caspian* and *Voyage of the Dawn Treader*)? What about a story about the creation of Narnia (*The Magician's Nephew*)?

Eventually there were seven books in the CHRONICLES OF NARNIA. If you haven't read them yet, today is a good day to begin!

Imagination is a gift from God and can be used in many ways to glorify Him.

FROM GOD'S WORD:
Then Jesus used stories [parables] to teach them many things (Matthew 13:3a, NCV).

LET'S TALK ABOUT IT:
1. How many different things in C. S. Lewis's own life (mentioned above) found their way into the Narnia stories?
2. Brainstorm different ways we can use our imaginations to bring glory to God.
3. Make up a parable—a story—to illustrate a truth from the Bible.

SAMSON OCCOM

Native-American "Moses"

Old Tomockham had built his wigwam in the Uncas Hills west of the River Thames in Connecticut many winters before his grandson Samson Occom was born in 1723. But by then, the once-powerful Mohegan tribe had dwindled to 351 struggling souls scattered in a few small villages on their ancient lands.

Samson's family lived a wandering life of hunting and fishing, occasionally trading with the English. White missionaries sometimes preached in his village and tried to teach the children to read, but most Indians listened only to receive a free blanket.

One day, however, the chief announced that he and his wife had become Christians. This encouraged more missionary visits, and Samson began paying attention. At the age of seventeen, he gave his life to Jesus and applied himself to learning to read the New Testament.

Not long after that, Rev. Eleazar Wheelock took an interest in Samson, teaching and encouraging him in his faith. But Wheelock's interest brought both blessings and problems as he arranged for Samson's education and guided him into missionary work. Wheelock's motives were mixed. He believed native missionaries would not only be more effective among the Indians but also cheaper. For two years the mission board paid Samson Occom nothing. When they finally set a salary, it was only a sixth of what they normally paid English missionaries. By then Occom was married with children. He had to spend most of his time hunting and fishing and selling crafts just to support them.

When Occom visited a Montauk village on Long Island, they agreed to support him if he would stay and set up a school. But rather than rejoice over this turn of events, Wheelock decided to send Occom to England to raise money for missions. Occom did well at this job, delivering more than three hundred sermons to crowds as large as three thousand people, and he brought back the huge sum of £12,000.

Occom arrived home, however, to find that Wheelock and the mission board had neglected his family and refused to share any money to support his future ministry. "I want you to go west," said Wheelock, "and take the Gospel to the Onondaga Indians in New York."

Occom hesitated. His people were suffering, not only for lack of a pastor but also from the abuse and corrupting influences of white society—disease, alcoholism, and the breakdown of family and tribal structures. Occom was also forty-five years old with weakening health, and Wheelock had not faithfully cared for his family during his earlier absence. But Wheelock did not accept these reasons. He accused Occom of being lazy and wanting more glory like he had received in England. The confrontation divided the two men.

Wheelock spent the missionary money Occom had raised to build Dartmouth College.

Ironically, Occom did go west, where he ended up doing his most important ministry. He recruited hundreds of Christian Indians from seven villages and led them to central New York, far beyond the bad influence of white society, to set up a peaceful Christian community in 1785 called Brothertown. Occom served as its minister, doctor, counselor, and spokesman until his death in 1792.

FORESIGHT
Creating Our Own Settlements

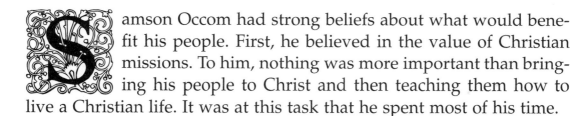amson Occom had strong beliefs about what would bene-
fit his people. First, he believed in the value of Christian
missions. To him, nothing was more important than bringing his people to Christ and then teaching them how to
live a Christian life. It was at this task that he spent most of his time.

However, he considered other things important, as well. The
world was changing for his people. Whites were increasing in number.
There was no stopping that. Some were kind toward the Indians, but
others took unfair advantage of them—taking their land without fair
payment, cheating them in trading, not paying fair wages. And always
there were whites that made these problems worse by offering the Indians liquor.

But there were other problems that accompanied both the good
and bad whites. The most obvious was disease. Whites brought ill-
nesses like measles against which the Indians had little resistance, and
many died.

But whites also introduced a different way of life. They wanted to
own land and farm it. Not only did this drive off much of the wildlife,

but once they had developed a farm, they weren't eager for Indians to set up camp on it for weeks at a time.

Even where whites welcomed Indians into their settlements, it often was not good for the Indians. Whites traded or bought many of the things that made their lives attractive—from hats and muskets to pots and furniture—but the animal skins and fish and handcrafts the Indians had to trade weren't valued as highly. They had to work much longer for things, leaving them poor and in need of charity.

"We need to get our people ready for this new way of life before they try to compete," Samson told his people. "We must end our nomadic life in the forest and settle down in villages and on farms to learn this new way of life, but we must not do it in the white villages. We must create our own settlements away from the whites for a time, and the only place to do that is in the west."

At that time, what Occom meant by "the west" was central New York, not the plains or the Rocky Mountains.

"In our own villages we can have schools for our children and churches," he urged the tribal elders. "We can maintain our tribal unity and establish self-government. If we don't do this, our people will be lost among the wave of white people."

"But if we move into villages," some of them complained, "we will forget the ways of the forest. We will not know how to hunt and fish."

"That may be true," he admitted, "but we cannot roam the forest forever. Many of us need to become farmers. Others can learn a trade as blacksmiths or carpenters. Some must learn how to build wagons and furniture. We need teachers and shopkeepers, surveyors and preachers. If we do not learn these skills, we will always be going to the whites with our hands out, and the evil ones among them will take advantage of us."

Slowly the tribal elders and many of the people from seven villages in New England agreed with Occom and made the trip west to establish a colony based on Christian principles. They named it Brothertown.

Foresight understands the future and prepares for it.

FROM GOD'S WORD:

The wise see danger ahead and avoid it, but fools keep going and get into trouble (Proverbs 22:3, NCV).

LET'S TALK ABOUT IT:

1. Why didn't Samson Occom just encourage his people to move west and continue their nomadic life of hunting and fishing?
2. Why might people not want to prepare for the future?
3. Tell about a time when you didn't prepare for the future and therefore missed out on something good. Is there something you should be doing *now* to prepare for *your* future?

CARING
Shepherd Through the Wilderness

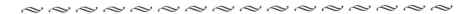

he American Revolution interrupted the New England Indians' movement west. Before the war began in 1776, an advance party had gone west to begin building Brothertown. But the rest had to wait in New England until peace returned in 1783.

Those who had gone west were not safe on the frontier during the war, so they drifted back toward home as refugees until they came to West Stockbridge, Massachusetts, where they were invited to stay with the Housatonic tribe until the war was over in 1783.

While in West Stockbridge, the Brothertown refugees made friends with their hosts, and they shared with them the vision of creating a community of their own beyond the current spread of the white settlements. When the war was over, several of the Stockbridge Indians accompanied the Brothertown Indians as they returned west to the land the Oneidas had given them. When they arrived, they immediately went to work on their half-finished houses, planted crops, and got the area ready for the arrival of their brothers and sisters from New England.

After the war, Sam Occom worked to prepare more families for the trip west. On May 8, 1784, he set out with the first group of new emigrants, traveling by ship down to New York and then up the Hudson River to Albany. At that point he entrusted the new emigrants to the care of Jacob Fowler to take them on to Brothertown.

He returned to New England and continued recruiting the next batch.

In the fall he brought another group west, this time traveling overland, visiting various Indian families along the way. He preached wherever he had opportunity, and there was scarcely an evening that he did not gather the people in some pioneer cabin.

He arrived at Brothertown near the end of October and continued going from cabin to cabin, encouraging the families and preaching each evening. On Thursday evening, November 3, 1785, he joined a happy couple in marriage.

In his diary, Occom reported that the couple and some of the other young people gathered in one house and then came in procession according to age to the house where the wedding was to take place. The old people seated themselves, and several Stockbridge Indians came, too.

After preaching a sermon on the nature of marriage and its honorableness, Occom had the couple hold hands while he led them in Christian marriage vows. After this he prayed and pronounced the couple husband and wife, and they all sang a marriage hymn.

Everyone sat down and ate a joyful marriage supper. After eating, the guests spent the rest of the evening singing "psalms and hymns and spiritual songs."

Though winter had set in, Occom's trip home was a missionary journey as well, preaching at every lodging place along the route.

Always concerned about the needs of his people, Occom made another trip to Brothertown in the spring to encourage his people and also to settle a dispute that had arisen with the Oneida Indians over the land. Year after year he walked back and forth between New England and Brothertown, 250 miles each direction, shepherding as many of his people as were desirous of moving west to their new home in central New York.

Caring requires going the extra mile.

FROM GOD'S WORD:
Shepherd God's flock. . . . Watch over them because you want to, not because you are forced. That is how God wants it. Do it because you are happy to serve, not because you want money (1 Peter 5:2, NCV).

LET'S TALK ABOUT IT:
1. What interrupted the migration from New England to Brothertown for seven years?
2. Why did Sam Occom make so many trips between New England and Brothertown?
3. Tell about a time when you were asked to care for someone—maybe a younger child. Were you able to "watch over them" because you were "happy to serve," or did you feel like you were forced to do it?

DIGNITY
"That's Not Fair!"

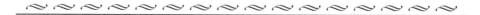

he land onto which Occom's New England Indians were settling had been given to them by the Oneida Indians of central New York in 1774. It was a strip some thirteen miles long and included over twenty-four thousand acres. Occom wisely recorded this gift and all the necessary legal papers with the secretary of state in Connecticut.

Only a few families managed to move and begin building Brothertown before the colonial war for independence broke out in 1776. Both the revolutionaries and the English (and even the French) tried to recruit the Indian tribes to their cause.

By letter, Occom urged his people to try to stay out of the war as much as possible. But he did go on to explain the nature of the American Revolution, concluding with this advice: "Now I think you must see who is the oppressor and who are the oppressed, and . . . if you must join on one [side] or the other, you can't join the oppressor but will help the oppressed."

Occom's followers tried to follow his advice, but some of the men—not having any other way to support their families—volunteered for the army, as did many of the Oneida Indians. Tragically many of these men were killed in the conflict.

By 1785 peace and stability had finally returned to the region. Whites began moving west, offering to buy Oneida land. Destitute because of the war, and with many of their men dead, the Oneidas were only too happy to sell, but they had earlier given away a huge portion of their excess land to the New England Indians. "You don't have that many people living here," they said to the Brothertown Indians, "so you don't need so much land."

"No," said Occom. "Your gift was very generous, but you can't take it back now." The Oneidas offered to let the Brothertown tribe keep 640 acres for those who were already there, but with the war over, the New England Indians were again starting to move west to fulfill Occom's plan of a settlement of their own. Next, the Oneidas said the New England Indians could come and live wherever they wanted, only they could not claim any special portion as their own.

Some of the New England Indians wanted to agree to this compromise, but Occom said no. "That would destroy the whole plan of having a designated settlement of our own. As a distinct people we would disappear if we agreed to that plan."

Finally the Oneidas surrendered all their land to the state of New York except a small reservation for themselves and a strip two miles wide and three miles long on which the Brothertown Indians had already settled. This smaller piece of land was only one sixth the size of the original gift.

Occom explained to a New York official, "The Oneidas can't give you our land. It's not theirs to give." Then he produced the document recorded years earlier in Connecticut.

In one of the very few times when an American governmental body honored Indian rights over what would benefit whites, the New York general assembly agreed with the terms of the 1774 land gift. All 24,052 acres belonged to the Brothertown tribe.

Having settled the land dispute, and having shepherded his

people west, Occom finally moved himself and his own family to Brothertown permanently in 1789. There he continued his pastoral work until he died on July 14, 1792.

The Brothertown community was relocated to Indiana in 1812 and again to Wisconsin in 1831. Today, the Brothertown Indian Nation of over twenty-two hundred members seeks recognition from the federal government as a unique tribe.

Dignity sometimes requires
standing up for your rights.

FROM GOD'S WORD:
But let justice flow like a river, and let goodness flow like a stream that never stops (Amos 5:24, NCV).

LET'S TALK ABOUT IT:
1. Why wasn't Samson Occom satisfied with the smaller piece of land the Oneidas offered his people?
2. How was Samson able to prove his people were being treated unfairly?
3. Tell about a time when something unfair happened to you. What did you do? How can we stand up for our rights in a way that produces dignity and respect?

JOHN G. PATON

———— ❦ ————

Missionary to the South Sea Islands

John Paton quit school as a young boy because of a cruel school-master. But he was determined to become a missionary, so he studied at home.

Born into a fine Christian home in Dumfries, Scotland, in 1824, John saved enough by the time he was twelve to pay for six weeks of private schooling. He continued to work his way through school, university, divinity school, and medical training. Finally, at the age of thirty-four, he was ordained by the Presbyterian Church of Scotland and commissioned as a missionary to the South Sea Islands.

On November 5, 1858, John and his wife, Mary, arrived on the Island of Tanna in the New Hebrides, a group of eighty islands now known as Vanuatu, about fifteen hundred miles northeast of Australia.

Other missionaries had established a solid work on Anatom, a southern island in Vanuatu, and several of their converts accompanied the Patons north to Tanna. At first the Patons felt overwhelmed by the warring cannibals of Tanna. Then they realized that the Christians from Anatom had been just as savage only a few years earlier.

The Tannese people worshiped and feared many idols and had no concept of a loving God. Witches and wizards in each village cast spells they claimed controlled life and death. They stirred up the people to drive out the missionaries.

Warfare between tribes worsened, with some of the worst fighting happening right outside the Patons' house.

Three months after arriving on Tanna, Mary Ann Paton gave birth to their son, Peter, but she became sick with fever and died on March 3. Their son also died from fever less than three weeks later. Paton was so shaken by these tragedies that he could hardly continue.

Not long after this, white traders—who also hated missionaries because they discouraged the natives from buying rum and muskets—deliberately sent three sick sailors among the people to spread measles, knowing that the witch doctors would blame Paton. The epidemic killed a third of the people, and the survivors sought revenge.

Two local chiefs protected Paton for a time, but that only increased the intertribal warfare. Soon Paton was running for his life, protected for a while by one chief, only to be chased by the same tribe the next day. He almost certainly would have been killed and probably eaten if a passing ship had not rescued him.

He had been on Tanna less than four years.

John then spent nearly two years speaking to churches in Australia and Scotland, raising financial support and recruiting more missionaries. One of those recruits, Margaret Whitecross, married John and returned with him to the islands in 1865.

John longed to settle again on Tanna, but the mission board assigned the Patons to Aniwa a few miles east. Superstitions on Aniwa were just as godless, but possibly because the island was smaller, there was less warfare and cannibalism. As the Patons learned the language, they slowly gained the people's confidence and were able to present the Gospel until nearly everyone on the island became a Christian.

In his later years, Paton traveled widely on behalf of missions until his death on January 28, 1906.

DEDICATION
Passing Up the Good to Achieve the Best

oung John Paton attended the school near his home in Dumfries, Scotland, and did well enough in his studies that his teacher took an interest in him and secretly gave him a suit of clothes. However, the man also had a terrible temper that exploded whenever one of his students displeased him.

One day after the teacher savagely beat John, he begged his mother, "Please don't make me go back. He whips children for no reason."

His mother looked into the incident and knew John had been treated unfairly, but she said, "You still need your education, John, and we cannot afford to send you to a private school. Give it one more try."

So John returned. But the moment the teacher saw him, he went into another rage and kicked John. In pain and terror, John ran for home.

Even though he was younger than twelve, there was nothing else for him to do but help in the family business of weaving stockings. He worked from six in the morning until ten at night with only a half hour off for breakfast and lunch and an hour off for dinner. But John did not waste those spare moments. He studied his lessons and saved his money so he could go to a private school.

John had already given his heart to Jesus and dedicated himself to becoming a missionary, and he knew that would require a good education.

Once he had saved enough, he enrolled in the Dumfries Academy for six weeks. Then he went to work for a surveying company that provided a shorter workday than helping with the stocking weaving at home. He studied during every available moment, including his lunch hour. His supervisor noticed the twelve-year-old's seriousness and offered him a promotion and special training if he would agree to serve the government for seven years.

"Thank you, sir," said John. "That is most kind." Then he stopped and considered. After seven years, he would be nineteen but not very far along in his preparation for mission work. "I'm sorry, I would agree for three or four years, but not for seven. That would put me too far behind in my preparations."

"Preparations for what, lad? Why would you refuse an offer that many gentlemen's sons would be proud of?"

"Because I have already dedicated my life to another Master."

The supervisor frowned. "And who would that be?"

"To the Lord Jesus," responded John, "so I must prepare as swiftly as possible to serve Him as a missionary."

"You fool!" the supervisor roared as he lunged toward John. "Accept my offer, or you are dismissed on the spot!"

John stood his ground. "Forgive me, I know you mean only kindness, but I cannot delay the purpose of my life. I cannot accept."

The angry supervisor paid John for the work he had done and fired him on the spot.

A less-dedicated youth might have gotten discouraged. But even though John was still so young, he went to the City of Glasgow, where he worked for the Presbyterian church part time as a visitor and tract distributor. Later he served as a street evangelist for Glasgow City Mission while he worked his way though the University of Glasgow, the Reformed Presbyterian Divinity School, and Andersonian College for medical training. Finally he felt ready to be a missionary.

Dedication is being set apart for a special task.

FROM GOD'S WORD:
The Holy Spirit said to them, "Set apart for me Barnabas and Saul to do a special work for which I have chosen them" (Acts 13:2b, NCV).

LET'S TALK ABOUT IT:
1. Do you think John was wise or foolish not to accept his supervisor's good job offer? Why?
2. It might seem *good* to go to the beach on Sunday morning, but it's *best* to go to church and worship God at that time. Think of two examples where you might have to give up something *good* in order to achieve the *best*.
3. Try inserting your names in the Bible verse above. For what special work has God chosen you?

RESOLVE

"It's God's Decision Whether Cannibals or Worms Eat My Body!"

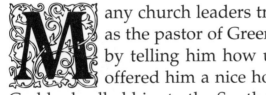any church leaders tried to convince John Paton to remain as the pastor of Green Street Church in Glasgow, Scotland, by telling him how useful he would be there. They even offered him a nice house and a larger salary, but he knew God had called him to the South Sea Islands.

"But the cannibals," warned an old gentleman. "You will be eaten by cannibals!"

He said it so often that John finally responded, "Mr. Dickson, you are old, and your body will soon be laid in its grave to be eaten by worms. What difference does it make if cannibals eat my body? Why should I save it for the worms? Isn't it more important to live and die serving and honoring the Lord Jesus?"

John had already resolved that since he had only one life to live, he was going to live it for Christ and leave the time, place, and means of his death in God's hands.

This freedom from the fear of death was essential on the Island of

Tanna, where witch doctors often tried to kill him. One day, when the tribal wars were raging, Paton held a worship service in a village.

"We don't need your God," said three powerful witch doctors. "If we ever get a piece of food you've eaten, we'll use it to kill you with magic."

"You think so?" said Paton. He then took some plums and called to the whole village, "Watch me eat this fruit."

He took a bite from each of the three plums and gave the witch doctors the remainder. The village people looked on in horror as the witch doctors began their magic rituals, wrapping the leftover fruit in leaves, burning part of them, and saying curses over them.

"What's taking so long?" said Paton. "Stir up your gods to help you! I'm not dead yet. In fact, I'm perfectly well!"

Finally they stopped and said, "We must wait until we call in other witch doctors to help us, but you will be dead within a week!"

"Very well," Paton said. "I challenge all your priests to unite in trying to kill me. But if I am still healthy a week from now, you must admit that your gods have no power over me and I am protected by the true and living God!"

Every day that week, the witch doctors blew their conch shell trumpets, rallying all the priests on the island to work their magic against the missionary, but on the next Sunday, John was healthy and strong as he stood before the whole village.

"My love to you all, my friends! I have come again to talk to you about the living God and His worship," announced Paton. "Come and sit down around me, and I will tell you about the love and mercy of my God and teach you how to worship and please Him."

Two of the witch doctors sat down with the people, but the third one, a very large, strong man, went off and came back with his spear.

"Of course he could kill me with his spear," said Paton to the crowd, "but that would not prove that his magic had any power. And if he does kill me with a spear, my powerful God who protected me from his magic will be angry with him."

For weeks thereafter, that witch doctor followed Paton through the jungle with his spear held high, but God prevented him from ever throwing it. John Paton, in the meantime, left the results in the hands of Jesus.

Resolve settles a matter so that you are not continually troubled by it.

FROM GOD'S WORD:
Choose for yourselves today whom you will serve. . . . As for me and my family, we will serve the Lord (Joshua 24:15, NCV).

LET'S TALK ABOUT IT:
1. What did John Paton mean when he asked Mr. Dickson, "Why should I save [my body] for the worms?"
2. How did Paton have the courage to challenge the witch doctors to try to kill him by magic?
3. Tell about a time when you resolved to trust and obey God. What challenges did you face? How did your resolve help you face those challenges?

INGENUITY
"Rain" From Below

The small island of Aniwa had no mountains to attract rain clouds or channel what rain did fall into streams, lakes, or rivers. Therefore, during the dry season there was no source of fresh drinking water. The people drank the milk of coconuts or stagnant water from the shrinking mud holes, often making themselves sick.

Even though the island was just sandy soil that had built up—at the highest point, no more than three hundred feet above its coral reef foundation—John Paton believed fresh water was trapped below the surface. But when he suggested digging a well, the native people laughed. "O 'Missi' [short for missionary], don't you know? Rain comes only from above, never from the ground."

"No," said Paton. "In my country fresh water comes springing up from the ground, and I hope to see it here, too." With that, he started digging and praying that if he found water it wouldn't be saltwater that had seeped in from the sea.

After Paton had been digging for a while, the oldest chief kindly said, "Missi, your head is going wrong. You are losing something! Don't let our people hear you talk about getting rain from below or they will never listen to your words again."

When Paton wouldn't stop digging, the old chief told his men, "Poor Missi! That's the way they all go crazy. They get an idea in their head that won't go away. What a shame! Keep watching him, and stop him if he tries to take his own life."

Paton kept digging. And when he got too tired, he hired some of the men to dig for him by paying them a fishhook for every three buckets of dirt they hauled up out of the well. That worked until a cave-in happened. It happened overnight when no one was in the hole, but the men would no longer go down, and Paton had to reinforce the walls with coral stones.

Days of grueling work resulted in a thirty-foot hole, and finally the sand began to feel damper and damper. One evening Paton climbed out of the hole and announced, "Tomorrow I think God will give us water from that hole!"

The old chief shook his head. "It won't be rain. If anything, you will drop through into the sea and be eaten by sharks!"

The next morning, in the sight of the assembled chiefs and their people, Paton prayed and climbed down into the well, taking with him a jug that everyone knew to be empty. In the center of the pit he sank a narrow hole some two feet deeper. Suddenly water began to gush up into the hole. It was muddy, but when he tasted it with shaking hands, it was fresh water—no salt!

Paton stood there in the bottom of the well with water rising around his ankles, praising God until the water had cleared. Then he filled his jug and climbed out of the well to present it to the oldest chief.

Everyone gathered around as the chief shook it, spilled a little into his hands, and finally tasted it. His eyes widened. "Rain! Rain! Yes, it *is* rain! But how did you get it?"

"I told you," said Paton with a grin. "God gave it to us out of His own earth. Go and see for yourselves!"

From that day on, the people had enough fresh water to drink, and they listened to Paton tell about the good God who loved and was eager to help them.

Ingenuity combines the wisdom to see a need and the intelligence to figure out a solution.

FROM GOD'S WORD:
God will use his wonderful riches in Christ Jesus to give you everything you need (Philippians 4:19, NCV).

LET'S TALK ABOUT IT:
1. Why did the native people think digging for "rain from below" was foolish?
2. What were the risks Paton took in digging the well?
3. Describe a time when you or someone in your family used ingenuity to solve a problem. Are you or your family facing a practical problem right now? Put your heads together and use some God-given ingenuity to solve it!

PANDITA RAMABAI

Liberator of Hindu Widows

Ramabai was born in 1858 to Hindu Chitpawan Brahmins, the highest caste (social class) in southern India. Her father, Anant Dongre, was a master of Sanskrit, the sacred language, and a teacher of the Hindu Scriptures. Men of lower caste and all women were forbidden to study the sacred language and texts—but Anant defied these prohibitions and taught both his wife and daughters. For this "sacrilege," the family was shunned by other Brahmins.

For years the family lived in poverty in the forest, but they continued their study of Hindu holy writings. Later, Anant and his family became traveling *puranikas*, reciting the Hindu scriptures in towns and villages and living off the gifts of grateful hearers. But years of hardship took their toll. When the region suffered a famine from 1876 to 1877, Ramabai saw first her father, then mother and sister weaken and die. Three years later her older brother also died of cholera.

In spite of severe restrictions on women of all castes, Ramabai began giving lectures on the education of women, commanding the respect of reform-minded Brahmins. Her intellect and knowledge were examined by a council of *pandits* ("teachers") in Calcutta and earned her the title of Pandita Ramabai.

But Ramabai still faced ridicule and opposition from orthodox

Brahmins, especially when she married a young lawyer beneath her caste. The couple was happy and had a daughter, Manorama ("Heart's Joy"). But in less than two years, Ramabai's husband died suddenly of cholera, leaving her a widow.

Disillusioned with her own religion, and always eager to learn, Ramabai explored the Christian faith. On a visit to England and America to study their educational methods, she wrote a book, *The High-Caste Hindu Woman*, breaking one thousand years of silence on the fate of widows in India. She also became a Christian and was baptized on September 29, 1883.

When she returned to India, she had a high purpose: "to show what great things God will do through one who is consecrated to His service." She established a home for high-caste Hindu widows, to rescue them from a life of abuse and train them as teachers of other women. The first home in Poona was called Sharada Sadan, "Abode of Wisdom," with room for fifty girls. After Ramabai rescued hundreds of suffering widows during a famine in central India in 1897, a second home was established thirty miles west at Kedgaon and named Mukti Sadan, "Place of Salvation."

Both homes were strictly neutral in matters of religion, but many of the Hindu women were attracted to Ramabai's Christian faith. Soon prayer meetings and Bible studies in Ramabai's rooms were filled, and many became Christians. In spite of severe opposition, the schools thrived and produced thousands of women who have served as evangelists, Bible women, and godly mothers.

Pandita Ramabai did more than anyone to call attention to the plight of India's widows and to create places of refuge and dignity. Few missionaries have led so many to faith in Christ. When she died on April 5, 1922, a telegram went around the world that said simply, "Ramabai promoted."

DIPLOMACY
The Disinvited Guests

 andita Ramabai watched the young Indian girl drawing water from the well and immediately recognized the signs of abuse—rope burns around the wrists, welts on her bare arms and legs. "What is your name?" Ramabai asked gently. But the startled girl scurried away with her water jar.

Ramabai followed and saw the house where the girl entered. Sucking in her courage, she knocked and asked to see the mistress of the house. Soon she was seated in a room filled with large leafy plants and blue and gold pillows. The girl she'd seen at the well poured tea. Ramabai tried to smile at her, but the girl only stared at her toes.

"We heard that you were home for a visit," beamed the mistress of the house. "Your aunt told us about your travels and how you've started a school! As for us, we have had nothing but bad luck. My son died, leaving me this worthless wife of his."

"I am sorry to hear about your son," said Ramabai. But it was the opening she needed. "I would like to take your daughter-in-law back with me to our school for widows. She—"

"That worthless girl?" scoffed Ramabai's hostess. "She's stupid . . . she does everything wrong. We have to beat her to get her to do anything. No, no."

Ramabai realized she'd have to use a more diplomatic approach. After a few more pleasantries, she rose to leave. "Please come to visit me in Poona, and bring your sister. We have several guest cottages at Sharada Sadan. The girl can come as your servant."

This idea appealed to the mistress of the house. "A holiday! Yes, yes, my sister and I will come!"

Not long after Ramabai returned to Poona, a bullock cart filled with baggage pulled up to the gate of Sharada Sadan. Ramabai smiled to herself. It looked like her guests planned to stay for a while. She showed them the guesthouse, filled with flowers, and a separate cookhouse where they could the rules of their caste.

Several weeks went by. The guests seemed to be enjoying themselves, and Ramabai never saw them strike the girl. *Good*, she thought. *Maybe they see that these girls should be treated with kindness.* But the girl still looked like a frightened deer and scurried off whenever Ramabai tried to talk to her.

But the mother-in-law had many questions. "Why do you let your students come and go wherever they like? I see them visiting your personal rooms! They should keep their place."

Ramabai smiled. "All their lives these girls have been treated as outcasts, have never been shown simple kindness. I wish them to see the contrast, the difference that love makes."

"You spoil them," muttered the woman.

One day Ramabai saw the girl dashing water onto her face again and again. Her eyes were red and puffy. "What is the matter?" Ramabai coaxed. "Please tell me."

The girl trembled but didn't run. Mouth quivering, she whispered, "They locked me in the cookhouse and put chili peppers on the fire . . . oh, my eyes! They sting so." Tears streamed down her face. "And . . . when you're not looking, they still beat me."

Ramabai's mouth set in a firm line. "Do you trust me, Little One? Will you stay with me if I send your mother-in-law and her sister away?"

The girl's eyes filled with fear, but she gave a slight nod.

That very day Ramabai appeared at the guesthouse. "Honored guests," she said with a humble bow. "Your visit is over. Thank you so much for coming. But your son's widow has chosen to stay here with us. Shall I send a boy to fetch a bullock cart?"

The mother-in-law opened her mouth to protest. But she knew that the girl was considered a woman by Hindu law and could not be legally forced to return with them. And by Hindu custom it was perfectly polite for a hostess to announce when a visit was over. The two women loaded their bags on the bullock cart, which lumbered off down the dirt road.

Ramabai watched them go, then drew the trembling girl close to her in a warm embrace. "You are safe here, Little One. Safe to live and love and learn. Shall we go find your new sisters?"

Diplomacy is finding a respectful way
to do the right thing.

FROM GOD'S WORD:
Patience can persuade a prince, and soft speech can crush strong opposition. (Proverbs 25:15).

LET'S TALK ABOUT IT:
1. Why did Ramabai invite the girl's mother-in-law to come to Sharada Sadan for a visit?
2. How did Ramabai show diplomacy?
3. Do you know someone who is diplomatic? How does that person find respectful ways to do the right thing?

COMPASSION
A New Year's Celebration

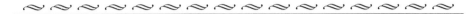

Thirteen-year-old Manorama had hardly slept for her excitement. Last night her mother had let her take Helen Dyer, the visiting English missionary, to the English "Watchnight" Service in Poona. Her mother, Pandita Ramabai, had stayed at Sharada Sadan, the school for Hindu widows, to lead a service in the Marathi language for the Christian girls. Now that it was morning—New Year's Day, 1895—they were taking Miss Dyer to a special breakfast at the home of one of the Christian teachers who lived in town.

Manorama felt very grown-up. She put on her *choli*, the short bodice that all Indian girls and women wore, then wrapped a long length of shimmery red cloth with gold trim around her waist to make a skirt. She added a matching piece as a shawl. "Happy New Year!" she said to Miss Dyer as she ran outside, where her mother was loading baskets onto a *dumnie*, a covered bullock cart. "Are we going to breakfast now, Mama?"

Pandita Ramabai smiled mysteriously. "Yes . . . but we have a few stops to make on the way. Where are the other girls I invited—oh, here they are."

Three excited schoolgirls climbed into the cart with Ramabai, Helen Dyer, and Manorama and snuggled among the baskets while a driver led the big white bulls through the hard-packed dirt streets. Soon the cart stopped. A sign said in English: *Anglo-Indian Children's Home.*

The girls scrambled out and helped carry a basket of treats into the home. Creamy brown children, some with brown eyes, others with gray or blue, clustered around them eagerly. "These children were abandoned on the street," Manorama heard her mother explain quietly to Miss Dyer. "Because they are mixed race, they are not wanted either by Indian families or English families—but they are wanted by God."

After handing out the treats and giving lots of hugs, the New Year's visitors climbed back into the cart, and the white bulls lumbered on down the streets of Poona. Soon they stopped again—this time at a government poorhouse. Manorama wrinkled her nose. The children's home was all right—but the poorhouse smelled bad, and many of the people were blind or crippled or sick. "Mama," she whispered, tugging on Ramabai's *sari*, "can't we just leave the basket and go on to our breakfast?"

Ramabai shook her head and continued to walk through the rooms, handing out the healthy treats made of lentils, butter, and sugar. "Poor things, they have no pleasures. We can give them our smiles."

Manorama was glad when they were back in the covered cart. But once more it stopped. Manorama groaned silently. This was the most unpleasant place yet—the lunatic asylum! Again Ramabai insisted on giving out the treats herself.

"If I let the keepers do it, some of the patients never get their share," she told her English friend. A wild-eyed man snatched his treat without any thank-you. Another pointed a finger at Miss Dyer and told her to go back to her own country. Others just rocked in a corner or stared blankly at the visitors. "I'm afraid many are here because opium and hashish [made from marijuana] have ruined their minds," said Ramabai sadly.

At last the New Year's visitors arrived at the home of their hostess. What a grand breakfast had been prepared for them! Rice-and-coconut custard, fried plantains, sliced fruit, and cakes were served on plantain leaves. As Manorama looked at all the wonderful food, she thought of the unwanted children, the poor, and the sick in body and mind they had just visited. She was sorry she had been so impatient. Pandita Ramabai had started the New Year in the best way—showing compassion to those less fortunate than themselves. And Manorama's mother had shown her something else—not to take her own blessings for granted.

Showing compassion to others helps us not take our own blessings for granted.

FROM GOD'S WORD:
This is what the Lord Almighty says: Judge fairly and honestly, and show mercy and kindness to one another (Zechariah 7:9).

LET'S TALK ABOUT IT:
1. Why do you think Pandita Ramabai took her daughter and several other girls along to deliver the New Year's baskets?
2. Showing compassion helps others, but how does showing compassion help *us*?
3. Think of someone less fortunate than you are. How could you show compassion to this person?

VISION
"Write My Name!"

andita Ramabai woke early. It was Easter morning, 1896. She looked tenderly at the fifteen girls from Sharada Sadan, her school for Hindu widows, sleeping in their makeshift tent under the trees. All had accepted Christ as Savior and eagerly begged to come to the yearly "camp meeting" where both Indian and English Christians from Poona and Bombay gathered each Easter to pray, worship, and hear preaching.

Ramabai slipped out of their tent and walked in the quiet woods, thanking God for her fifteen spiritual children. As the sun rose, filling the woods with a dappled brilliance of green and gold, Ramabai's heart was full of love for her heavenly Father. Suddenly she prayed, "Gracious God, give me two hundred and twenty-five more spiritual children before the next camp meeting!"

Later Ramabai wondered whether she should pray such a prayer. After all, she had room for only fifty girls at Sharada Sadan! And the local Hindu priests had written the parents and told them to take their girls out of the school when they heard that some had become Christians. So the number of students had actually gone *down* in the last few months. But in her heart, Ramabai knew that God had given her a vision—a big vision—to reach out to hundreds more young Hindu widows, even though she had no idea where she would put them.

As spring turned into summer, word reached Poona that central India was suffering a great famine. Ramabai's heart ached. She remembered the famine that had taken the lives of her father and mother and sister. She knew what it was like to chew grass, hoping to fill the ache in her stomach. She remembered being so weak she could hardly stand or walk. And during a famine, orphans and widows who had no one to protect them were often in moral danger in the relief camps.

Now Ramabai knew why God had given her the vision of hundreds of girls coming to her school. She must go to central India to rescue suffering widows and orphans from the streets and gutters.

Leaving Sharada Sadan in the capable hands of her assistant, Soonderbai Powar, Ramabai and a "Bible woman" began their rescue mission. When Ramabai had found ten or twenty girls willing and able to make the journey, she sent them back to Poona by train with the Bible woman. The students at Sharada Sadan took on the task of welcoming the pathetic creatures that stumbled off the train.

But bubonic plague was creeping through southern India, and the local magistrate made a rule that Sharada Sadan could not add any more students. What was Ramabai going to do with all the young girls sleeping in tents all over the school grounds?

The fruit farm! Of course. Ramabai had bought the farm hoping to help feed her students and make them self-sufficient. No buildings had been built there—yet. But Pandita Ramabai moved all the famine victims to the farm thirty miles west of Poona.

When harvest finally arrived in 1897, the food emergency in central India was over. The rescue missions stopped. Ramabai counted the girls who had made their way to her school. Not 225 . . . but 300!

Ramabai shared the Good News about Jesus with the girls, many of whom were from the lower castes. When a missionary visited the school and held special services, sixty-seven girls gave their hearts to

Christ. The services continued, more accepted Christ . . . and on November 15, 1897, seventeen carts holding seven or eight girls each made a procession to the Bheema River five miles away for baptism.

As Pandita Ramabai wrote down the name of each girl who wanted to be baptized, a little girl of six tugged at her skirt. "Bai, Bai, write my name!"

The tiny widow was carried into the river and baptized in the name of the Father, the Son, and the Holy Spirit. No wonder Pandita Ramabai's second school for widows was named Mukti Sadan—"Place of Salvation."

When God gives us a vision of what He wants us to do for Him, He will make a way for us to do it.

FROM GOD'S WORD:
O Sovereign Lord! You have made the heavens and earth by your great power. Nothing is too hard for you! (Jeremiah 32:17).

LET'S TALK ABOUT IT:
1. Why do you think Ramabai went to rescue young widows from the famine even before she had a place to put them?
2. How did God turn obstacles (problems) into stepping-stones to accomplish Ramabai's vision?
3. Has God given you a vision for something BIG—but you don't know how it can be done? Take *one step* toward your vision, and see if God shows you the next step . . . and the next.

JOY RIDDERHOF

―――――――――――― ❧ ――――――――――――

Founder of Gospel Recordings

Joy Ridderhof had been working as a missionary for six years in Central America in the 1930s when a severe case of malaria sent her home to Los Angeles. As she lay weak and feverish in bed in her attic room, she fretted about the new converts she had left behind in a remote village in the mountains of Honduras, many of whom could not read the Spanish Bible.

But everyone in Honduras, it seemed, loved recorded music. What if she made a record with music and the gospel message in Spanish? She was sure the novelty of it would draw a crowd, and the villagers could hear God's Word even when no missionary was present.

Even in her sickness, Joy's excitement grew. There were people all over the world who did not have the Bible in their own language. But anyone could *listen* to the Good News if it was recorded in his or her own language. . . .

The idea for Gospel Recordings was born.

In 1944 Joy and her friend Ann Sherwood set out on their first recording trip—a ten-month tour in Mexico and Central America. The travel to remote mountain villages was often difficult, and the work required endless patience. For each dialect they had to find a tribesman who knew English to help translate the gospel scripts—often by simply repeating the words Joy spoke, phrase by phrase. They had to carry heavy recording equipment, including a generator to make their own electricity. But they were able to record gospel messages in thirty-five new dialects.

A second trip in 1947 took them to Alaska, visiting remote Indian tribes. In 1949 they sailed for the Philippine Islands. (See the TRAIL-BLAZER BOOK *Race for the Record*.) Sometimes it took two or three different people to translate from English to one language, then from that language into the desired dialect. But now they had a compact, battery-run recorder, and they went home with ninety-two new languages!

On Joy and Ann's fourth recording trip, they were joined by Sanna Barlow and headed for Australia and islands in the Pacific, followed by a trip to Asia and Africa.

Back in Los Angeles, the home staff of Gospel Recordings kept busy producing the recordings, handling the mailing, and developing new equipment that could be used in remote areas of the world. But it was prayer and vision that upheld the ministry no matter what difficulties arose. Stories poured in from all over the world of men and women, boys and girls, who heard the message of God's love for the first time and gave their hearts and lives to Jesus because of these gospel recordings.

Even though Joy Ridderhof died in 1984, the work of Gospel Recordings continues. GR offices in over twenty countries continue to produce records in new languages and dialects sent to them by field recordists. To date, over forty-nine hundred languages and dialects (out of eight thousand known languages) have been captured on records, taking the Gospel all over the world—all because one woman said "Yes!" to God.

REJOICING
"GRP—Good Rejoicing Practice!"

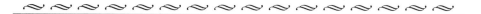

The four Sutherland children stood on the pearl white sandy beach, gaping at the two American women as they waded to shore from the small boat. The interisland steamer that had brought Joy Ridderhof and her teammate, Ann Sherwood, to Brooke's Point on Palawan Island in the Philippines was anchored farther out in the shallow bay.

"Welcome! Welcome! Here at last!" boomed Mr. Sutherland, the Scottish Brethren missionary who had eagerly written Gospel Recordings, begging them to come. "And don'na mind the children's stares— the two wee ones hav'na seen white women before, other than their ain mither."

Soon all the recording equipment and luggage had been deposited on the beach, then taken by *carabao* cart to the Sutherland home tucked among the graceful palm trees along the shore. People from the town kept popping in to greet the two women. "You've come at last!" "We've been waiting for you!" "We're so glad you've come!"

Joy and Ann looked at each other, bewildered and amused.

"We've never come to record anyplace where we've been so . . . so *expected*."

"Aye. From the first time we heard about you, we knew Gospel Records was the answer for how to reach the mountain tribespeople on Palawan. They have no written language, so of course they have no Bibles. But a few speak Tagalog, the trade language."

"Mama even translated some songs into Palawano," chirped one of the sandy-haired Sutherland children, "and a quartet of girls has practiced the music!"

Joy's heart sang. God had truly prepared the way!

The next day Ann set up the recorder in the chapel, where the recording would take place. A Palawano man who spoke Tagalog was waiting patiently. The Filipino girls were practicing their songs. Ann flipped the On switch . . . but nothing happened.

"It always works in the end," Joy said confidently. "Let's rejoice for what God is going to do!"

But the recorder stayed silent all that day.

"I call this GRP—Good Rejoicing Practice!" said Joy. "That's the way we overcome the difficulties Satan puts in our path. Let's not be discouraged."

Each day Ann Sherwood fiddled with the machine, taking out tubes, wiggling wires. But nothing helped. When the steamer came back for them three days later, not one gospel message had been recorded.

Joy could hardly bear to see the disappointment on the faces of the Sutherland family as they waved good-bye. "Rejoice . . ." she whispered to herself. But never had it seemed so hard.

As they steamed north, a fellow passenger casually mentioned a Palawanos boy who was at a Farm School near Puerto Princesa, the largest town on Palawan. Joy jotted his name in her notebook: "Lastani . . . Farm School . . ." Mrs. Sutherland had also told her that some of the Filipino girls who had practiced the Palawanos songs were going to school in Puerto Princesa. Joy made another note.

In Puerto Princesa, the recorder spent a day in a repair shop and came back working—off and on, but working. By that time, Lastani had been contacted and got permission to leave the Farm School to record the scripts—directly from English into Palawanos! The girls from Brooke's Point were contacted and were delighted to get a chance to record their songs after all.

"This Lastani is a much better translator than the dear fellow back in Brooke's Point," Ann murmured, listening to the Palawanos boy read flawlessly.

Joy beamed. "God knew we needed some 'rejoicing practice' before He showed us that He had an even better plan!"

Rejoicing even when things go wrong helps us put our faith in God, not in our circumstances.

FROM GOD'S WORD:
Rejoice in the Lord always. Again I will say, rejoice! (Philippians 4:4, NKJV).

LET'S TALK ABOUT IT:
1. Why do you think Joy wasn't discouraged when the recorder didn't work?
2. How does rejoicing affect your mood? Your attitude? Your faith?
3. Name something that seems to be going wrong right now in your life. Instead of complaining and being down-in-the-mouth, could this be an opportunity for GRP—Good Rejoicing Practice?

PATIENCE
Raining Orchids

~~~~~~~~~~~~~~~~~~~~~~~~~~~~~~~~~~~

Joy Ridderhof and Ann Sherwood stood in the muddy road and looked at the neat little bamboo house standing on stilts. "Here we go again," Ann joked, "announcing to total strangers that we've come to stay with them."

The two women had come to the island of Mindoro in the Philippines to make gospel recordings for the Mangyan tribe—if they could find them. Joy and Ann set out for the town of Bongabong, which was closest to the mountains where the Mangyan tribespeople lived. They had the name of a Protestant Filipino family, the Sulits, who lived near Bongabong. Joy hoped they were home—it looked like rain again.

A stream of children poured out of the house and scrambled down the bamboo ladder to welcome their visitors, followed by their somewhat bewildered parents. But when Mr. and Mrs. Sulit discovered that Joy and Ann were Christians, their faces lit up. "Of course you must stay with us," said Mr. Sulit in careful English.

"I counted *nine* children," Ann whispered to Joy as they followed their hosts up the ladder.

As Mrs. Sulit served tea to her guests, Joy explained their mission.

Mr. Sulit shook his head sadly. "We are so sorry. We cannot help you. We rarely see any Mangyans. They are afraid of the villages, and now that the rainy season is here, they rarely come down from the mountain."

"But we have asked God to send them to us," Joy explained patiently. "Would you keep a lookout for them?"

Nine little Sulits were dispatched to keep an eye on the road while Joy and Ann continued to visit with their hosts. They had been there less than an hour when the cry went up outside: "Mangyans! Mangyans!"

The Sulits and the two American women rushed to the door. Sure enough, two teenage boys wearing only loincloths were coming down the road headed for Bongabong, their arms full of wild orchids to sell.

Mr. Sulit approached the boys gently so as not to scare them off. Joy watched as the boys gave him the orchids, then followed him into the yard. He must have offered to buy all their flowers.

Mr. Sulit looked up at the American women on the porch. "One of them speaks Tagalog—that is why he was sent to town to sell the orchids," he said with wonder.

It took quite a bit of translating back and forth from Joy to Mr. Sulit to the teenage boy and back again to explain what they wanted the boys to do. But the boys seemed willing (they'd sold all their flowers, after all!) and squatted down inside the house as Ann set up the recorder.

Patiently Joy said a sentence from her gospel script in English, which Mr. Sulit translated into Tagalog, and then encouraged the boy to say it in the Mangyan language. Each time the boy spoke a phrase, Ann turned the recorder on to capture it on tape. Then, just to be sure he was translating the phrase correctly, they played the phrase back to him, and he translated it back into Tagalog, and Mr. Sulit translated it back into English.

On, off. On, off. All that day and the next. English . . . Tagalog . . . Mangyan; then Mangyan . . . Tagalog . . . English.

Joy and Ann were tired and sore from bending over the tape

recorder for so many long hours when the teenage boys finally waved good-bye and headed back toward the mountains. But they had recorded enough gospel messages to create four records—two sides each—to reach the Mangyans with the Good News about Jesus.

"Hmm. Now all we need is a simple, hand-crank record player that doesn't need batteries," mused Joy thoughtfully as they headed for a different village, a different tribe.

Doing a job well is sometimes tedious and requires patience to see it through.

FROM GOD'S WORD:
Let us not become weary in doing good, for at the proper time we will reap a harvest if we do not give up (Galatians 6:9, NIV).

LET'S TALK ABOUT IT:
1. Why do you think Joy Ridderhof bothered to check what the boy had translated, even though it meant taking twice as long?
2. What do you think kept Joy and Ann going when the job of making a recording took a long time or got boring?
3. Think about a job or task you have a hard time finishing. Is it boring? Does it take too long? Ask yourself: What are the benefits of finishing this job? Keep your eye on the goal and see if it helps you have patience.

BOLDNESS
A Wounded Head Under a Hairy Scalp

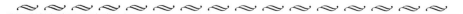

he Gospel Recordings trio—Joy Ridderhof, Ann Sherwood, and Sanna Barlow—had been traveling in Africa for many months. But everyone discouraged them from going to Ethiopia. *"The political situation is very touchy here,"* a missionary wrote. *"The Minister of Education banned the gospel records you sent us in the Amharic language."*

But Joy was reading Psalm 68: *"Ethiopia will quickly stretch out her hands to God."*[3]

"How much money do we have?" Joy asked her companions. All three women emptied their pockets and purses. Just enough to cover one plane ticket to Addis Ababa. Joy made up her mind. She would go to Ethiopia and see for herself.

The missionaries who met her at the plane tried to caution her. "The emperor is surrounded by people who are very hostile to Christianity. If you tried to contact tribespeople or make gospel recordings here, you would immediately be under suspicion—and so would anyone who helped you."

---

[3]Psalm 68:31 (NKJV).

Joy thought about that. "Then," she said, tilting her chin stubbornly, "I must visit the emperor himself and get his permission."

She contacted the American ambassador, Dr. Simonson. The ambassador shrugged. "I will try to get you an audience with the emperor, but I can't promise anything."

Then word came: She had an appointment to meet with His Imperial Majesty, Haile Selassie, Emperor of Ethiopia. Joy was ecstatic! Except she had one little problem—whatever would she *wear* to meet the king?

The appointed day arrived. Joy, wearing a borrowed suit, hat, and gloves, arrived at the palace with Ambassador Simonson, solemn and dignified in his formal swallow-tail coat. She was instructed how to enter the hall: Bow low, walk slowly, never turn your face away from the emperor. The minister of education would act as interpreter.

To Joy's surprise, Emperor Haile Selassie was surprisingly open as she explained her request. He believed in the Bible, he said. Yes, he would be pleased if she would make recordings in languages of people who could not read.

Joy was elated. She bowed and backed slowly out of the room, then turned happily to the minister of education. "Will you please give me a written letter of the emperor's permission?"

"What permission?" said the minister of education coldly.

The door that had opened a crack slammed shut again. Joy knew she could not proceed with just the *verbal* word of the emperor. She had to have it in writing.

She flew back to Nairobi, Kenya, with no recordings. But she wasn't discouraged. Not Joy. She read and reread Psalm 68. It was God's promise! She also noticed a strange phrase in verse 21: "But God will wound the head of His enemies, the hairy scalp of the one who still goes on in his trespasses [sins]." She didn't know what *that* meant, but she would leave that to God.

Just before her team was scheduled to leave Africa, Joy applied once more for visas to enter Ethiopia. To her surprise, the applications were approved—for three months! The trio looked at one another in amazement. She had been told it would be a few days at most. Three months later they had recorded over thirty languages! But Joy was still curious. What had happened to open the door?

"Oh," one of the missionaries told her, "the minister of education developed a strange mental condition and had to leave the country for treatment. Since he's been gone, a lot of the restrictions against Christianity have lifted."

Joy grinned. Sounded like a "head wound" under a "hairy scalp" to her.

*Confidence in God's promises gives us the boldness
we need to speak to governors and kings.*

FROM GOD'S WORD:
I will speak of Your testimonies also before kings, and will not be ashamed (Psalm 119:46, NKJV).

LET'S TALK ABOUT IT:
1. Why did Joy Ridderhof decide to talk directly to the emperor?
2. Why didn't she get discouraged even when the minister of education continued to put obstacles in her way?
3. Name some of God's promises from the Bible. How can these promises help you to be bold for God?

RÓMULO SAUÑE

An Inca With a Royal Message

Why did the World Evangelical Fellowship give its first-ever Religious Liberty Award to Rómulo Sauñe (pronounced ROW-muh-low SOUW-nyay), a humble Quechua Indian pastor from the Peruvian Andes? Christians from Africa, Asia, Europe, the Middle East, Latin America, and North America gathered in Manila, Philippines, on June 23, 1992, to honor him because of his courageous ministry while his life was threatened by Communist terrorists. These terrorists had already murdered his grandfather, assaulted and beaten his grandmother and left her for dead, burned down his family home twice, and destroyed his church.

In an attempt to take over the South American country of Peru, these same terrorists, calling themselves the Shining Path, murdered at least twenty-five thousand people, including four thousand Christians and five hundred pastors. Thousands of other civilians were caught in the cross fire and killed as the government tried to stop the terrorists and capture their leader, Abimael Guzmán Reynoso.

Ten weeks after Pastor Rómulo received his award in Manila, he traveled to his childhood mountain village of Chakiqpampa, where he encouraged the Christians and visited his grandfather's grave. On September 5, 1992, as Rómulo drove back down to the city of Ayacucho, the Shining Path set up a roadblock and attacked again, this time killing Rómulo, his brother, two nephews, and several other people. When the guerrillas checked the bodies and found that they had killed Rómulo Sauñe, one radioed to his commander, "We got him!" Then they left.

Rómulo Sauñe had been born on January 17, 1953, in Chakiqpampa, where as a young boy he herded sheep on the steep mountains and learned of his Inca ancestors. Through his mother's side of the family, he may have descended from the royal Inca priesthood. Nevertheless, first Rómulo's uncle and then his grandfather, Justiniano Quicaña, accepted the Gospel of Jesus and became Christians. Other family members followed, including young Rómulo, until there was a thriving church in their village, a church that sent out missionaries to all the surrounding villages.

In 1978, realizing that the denominational divisions between Christians introduced by various outside mission organizations hurt the gospel witness, Rómulo led in the formation of a joint mission association, TAWA, which restored unity to the Christians and helped translate the Bible into the Quechua language. This task was completed on September 3, 1987, and within a short time forty thousand copies were sold to the people.

In time Rómulo became a pastor of the pastors, guiding and encouraging them as the Shining Path became more and more violent.

Rómulo's death, however, did not go unnoticed. Braving the threats of the Shining Path, two thousand people paraded through the streets of Ayacucho singing "Onward Christian Soldiers" and carrying banners declaring "Ayacucho for Christ" and the Bible verse, "For to me, to live is Christ and to die is gain" (Philippians 1:21, NIV).

One week later, government agents finally captured Guzmán and his top lieutenants, bringing an end to the worst of the Shining Path's reign of terror (though the organization still exists and sometimes launches terrorist attacks).

LOVE
Heart Medicine

any of the Shining Path revolutionaries who followed Abimael Guzmán were Rómulo Sauñe's age, poor Indians from small villages like his own. Guzmán, who had been a university professor, realized that it would be impossible to persuade most people to join his revolution, so he chose a simpler path: terror. His soldiers would enter a village and ask for volunteers. If the young men did not step forward to join, the Shining Path soldiers would begin killing the women and children. Of course, the next village would hear about the massacre, and the men would more quickly "volunteer" when the Shining Path soldiers came to their town.

Juan was one of these soldiers. He had also been a childhood friend of Rómulo.

One day the two old friends met on the streets of Ayacucho, and Rómulo invited Juan to step into a café and have a soda while they caught up on old times.

After Rómulo told how God was working in his life, how the Bible translation had been completed, how the churches were coming together, he asked Juan what he'd been up to.

"I've joined the Shining Path," Juan boasted. "We've got some great new weapons, and we're taking over the country. You ought to join us, Rómulo."

"Hmm. These weapons of yours, you ever use them?"

"Oh yes. We get good training."

"No. I mean, have you ever used them on *people*?"

Juan's eyes, which had sparkled with so much enthusiasm only a few moments before, dimmed, and his gaze dropped to his lap. "Yes," he admitted in not much more than a whisper. "The other night we went into a village, and my leader insisted that we kill even the women and children."

Juan fell quiet, and Rómulo recalled how other Shining Path members had beaten his grandmother and burned their house. His one-time friend had joined his enemies. Still, he prayed silently for Juan while the young man tried to swallow the lump in his throat. Finally Juan looked up. "It's been tearing out my heart ever since!"

"Yes, yes. I think you need some heart medicine, Juan."

"But what can help this?" He grabbed his chest as tears threatened to overflow.

"Only Jesus has the power to forgive you for such violence. What you need is the love of Christ to fill your life. Look!" And Rómulo opened his Quechua New Testament and showed Juan how the blood of Jesus cleanses us from all sin (1 John 1:7) and how God could give him a new life in Christ.

"Can I do that now?" Juan asked.

"Yes," Rómulo assured him, and together they prayed as Juan joined a new army with weapons of peace and love.

Juan was just one of many young rebels that Rómulo led out of the Shining Path's violence and darkness and into Christ's wonderful light (1 Peter 2:9).

Jesus' kind of love cares even for our enemies.

FROM GOD'S WORD:
God showed his great love for us by sending Christ to die for us while we were still sinners (Romans 5:8).

LET'S TALK ABOUT IT:
1. Why did Rómulo think Juan needed some heart medicine?
2. Why do you think Rómulo wanted to help Juan even though Juan was part of a group that killed even women and children?
3. Do *you* have an "enemy" (someone who has hurt you in some way) who needs to hear about God's "heart medicine"? Ask God to help you love your enemy the same way Jesus loved us even while we were still sinners.

BOLDNESS
Angels Watching Over You

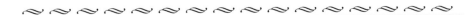

e may not understand why God allowed the Shining Path to murder Rómulo Sauñe, but it wasn't because God can't protect His people. For instance, late one night, a knock had come on Rómulo's door.

"Who's there?"

"Is the pastor in?"

The local pastor for this town was not there at that time, so Rómulo said, "No. He is not here." Normally he would have quickly offered to help anyway because he was a pastor, but something kept him silent. After a moment, he heard footsteps walking away.

Why hadn't Rómulo opened the door? Was he too tired? Didn't he care? Maybe the man wanted to hear about Jesus.

The next morning another knock came on the door, and this time Rómulo opened it to find a man with a sack over his shoulder. "Are you Rómulo Sauñe?" the man said.

When Rómulo nodded, the man asked, "Why didn't you answer the door last night?" Rómulo didn't have a good reason, but the man explained. "Two Shining Path comrades and I came to kill you, but when no one opened the door, we left. All night I couldn't sleep," he admitted. "I know I was wrong."

Rómulo took this opportunity to tell the man about Jesus. Together they prayed, then the man opened his sack and gave Rómulo the gun and ammunition he had intended to use to kill him the night before.

In another situation the Shining Path entered a village in the Andes. "Who's the leader here?" they demanded.

The pastor, a poor Indian believer named Jorge, stepped forward, trembling.

"Are you willing to accept the authority of the Shining Path in this village?" the rebel demanded.

In spite of his fear, Jorge said, "The Lord is my authority. There is no other."

The rebel leader laughed and turned to the villagers. "This man isn't fit to be your leader. We will make an example of him."

They tied Jorge to a chair and attached dynamite to its legs, then lit the fuse and ran for cover. The dynamite exploded, and the villagers began to wail with grief, but when the smoke and dust cleared, there sat Pastor Jorge, alive and unharmed.

As the people cheered and praised God, the terrorists fled the village.

In another village near the edge of the jungle, the Christians were meeting for prayer when the Shining Path surrounded their church. "Come out with your hands up!" the rebel leader yelled.

"Wait, let's pray," the pastor urged when the believers began to panic. "God will protect us."

After the people fell to their knees, crying out for His protection, the rebels fired a few warning shots and yelled, "Come out now, or we will shoot you all!"

Within the church, a tall man dressed in a uniform suddenly stood up from a chair and made his way toward the door. Even though this was a small village where everyone knew everyone else, no one recognized him. There had been only about fifty people in the church, all sitting, talking, and praying together. Surely they would have noticed a stranger among them, and yet no one remembered seeing him until he stood up.

The stranger drew his pistol and opened the door. Then he just stood there with his gun pointed up. After a moment of silence, the Shining Path terrorists began screaming and running out of town.

When they were gone, the stranger put away his gun and walked calmly off into the night. No one ever saw him again.

Boldness relies on the Lord for deliverance.

FROM GOD'S WORD:
He orders his angels to protect you wherever you go (Psalm 91:11).

LET'S TALK ABOUT IT:
1. Why do you think Rómulo didn't answer the door in the middle of the night?
2. Who do you think the tall stranger was who scared away the rebels around the church?
3. Have there been times when you were afraid to be bold about your faith? What did you think might happen? What did you do (or not do)? What would you like to happen the next time you are in that situation?

FRIENDLINESS
The Helper on the Mountain

ómulo Sauñe, his grandfather, and the other members of his family first heard the Gospel from a Spanish Bible. But the mountain Indians mostly spoke Quechua, so it was hard to understand the Spanish Bible.

Rómulo thought about Romans 10:14: *"How can they believe in the one of whom they have not heard?"* (NIV).

He was determined to bring the good news of the Gospel to his people, but he realized an important tool would be getting the Bible translated into his native Quechua language. So with the support of TAWA (the association of Peruvian churches), a team from Wycliffe Bible Translators and Rómulo set to work.

Rómulo had received his training at the Latin American Bible Institute in Los Angeles. While in the States, he had met and married his wife, Donna.

But knowing that the revolution was spreading across his country and that the Shining Path often targeted pastors and churches, Rómulo was concerned that the people have Bibles of their own that they could read and understand even if there was no pastor or if it became too dangerous to meet together. So they worked hard.

But in spite of the skills of the translation team, some concepts were hard to communicate in Quechua without knowing more about the culture and geography of the Holy Land. Rómulo wanted to know, for instance, what Mount Sinai was like.

"What difference does it make?" asked the other members of the translation team. "It's just a big mountain."

"Well," explained Rómulo, "it makes a lot of difference. In English or Spanish or Hebrew there are only a few words—hill, mountain, peak, foothill—but in Quechua we have dozens. One can't just say, 'mountain.' I need to understand the appearance and altitude."

Again and again translation problems arose that required the first-hand insight that no one on the team had. "If I could walk through the Holy Land and see it with my own eyes," Rómulo lamented, "then we could get it right."

Then one day a letter arrived from a woman in Texas. In it was $2,000, enough to pay for a trip to the Holy Land.

When Rómulo arrived in Israel, the sights and sounds of the countryside brought the Bible to life. The dry and rocky terrain was similar to parts of Peru. He could describe it with words his people would understand. But there was no one to explain other things to him in a language he could understand. He tried English, but he wasn't that good at speaking it. He felt discouraged. This was where he needed to be, but he needed help. With determination, he kept on, and one day while climbing Mount Carmel, a man dressed in Arab-style clothing joined him.

Even though he was discouraged, Rómulo greeted the man with a friendly smile, and speaking the few words of Hebrew he had learned, he told the man that he was from South America. Suddenly the man responded in Spanish and began explaining all the sights to Rómulo and answering his many questions. On and on they walked, discussing the ancient biblical events that had taken place in the area.

The man seemed to know all the facts.

Finally they came to a fork in the trail, and the man said good-bye.

How joyful Rómulo was that he had finally found someone with whom he could communicate easily. He looked back to wave one last time, but there was no one in sight even though the trail could be seen for some distance.

Could it be, thought Rómulo, *that God sent an angel to encourage me?*

Friendliness opens the door to greater things.

FROM GOD'S WORD:
Remember to welcome strangers, because some who have done this have welcomed angels without knowing it (Hebrews 13:2, NCV).

LET'S TALK ABOUT IT:
1. Why was Rómulo determined to get the Bible translated into the Quechua language?
2. How did the man he met on Mount Carmel help him?
3. Tell about a time when you were friendly to someone and received an unexpected blessing in return. Do you think it might have been an angel in disguise?

WILLIAM J. SEYMOUR

"Father" of Modern Pentecostals

When William Seymour was a boy, he often imagined seeing God. He was born on May 2, 1870, in Centerville, Louisiana, to Simon and Phyllis Seymour, former slaves, who raised him as a Baptist. But Sunday school wasn't enough. William studied the Bible on his own to check out whether his visions of God were true.

At the age of twenty-five, William moved to Indianapolis, where he worked as a railroad porter and a waiter in a fashionable restaurant and attended a black Methodist Episcopal church.

In 1900 he moved to Cincinnati, Ohio, and enrolled in a holiness Bible school. There he studied sanctification (how God makes us holy), healing, and the expectation that there would be a worldwide revival in the Holy Spirit before the Lord's soon return.

Seymour heard God call him to become a preacher, but he resisted until he caught smallpox, an often-deadly disease. William recovered but lost the sight in one eye due to infection. Having been so sick, he realized that one should be quick to obey God's call. So he immediately accepted ordination as a preacher.

One day William Seymour received a letter from a small church in Los Angeles. One of its members had heard Seymour preach, and the church invited him to be their pastor. A train ticket was included in the letter.

At the new church in southern California, Seymour preached that the Holy Spirit (or Holy Ghost, as He was often called) was eager to baptize every believer with power just like what was reported in the book of Acts. After a month of intense prayer and fasting, in April 1906 the Holy Spirit fell in power on the small group, and several members spoke in tongues. The experience was like fire, spreading so quickly that huge crowds began coming every day and every night to the mission at 312 Azusa Street. People were healed of sickness, hundreds were converted to Christ, and many were sent out as missionaries around the world. (See the TRAILBLAZER BOOK *Journey to the End of the Earth*.)

This powerful move of the Spirit became known as the Azusa Street Revival. Within two years, the movement took root in over fifty nations. Today, the spiritual heirs of the Azusa Street Revival number over half a billion people, making Pentecostals and Charismatics (as they are often called) the second largest and the fastest-growing family of Christians in the world. It includes the Church of God in Christ, the Assemblies of God, Apostolic Church, Four Square Church of God, and numerous other denominations and independent "full Gospel" churches. Whether black or white, Hispanic or Asian, almost all churches in this movement can trace their roots directly or indirectly to the humble mission at 312 Azusa Street and its pastor, William J. Seymour.

DISCERNMENT
The Headless Phantom

urrying home alone one night, young Willie Seymour thought he would save a little time by taking a short-cut ... through a cemetery. The boy stepped through a hole in the fence but found it hard to see any distinct path. In the dark he weaved his way between the gravestones, trying not to trip over low ones that might be hidden in the grass.

He had just come around a tree when he noticed a shape a short distance ahead of him. Unlike the tall gravestones that appeared a bluish gray in the moonless night, this shape was dark and about as tall as a man.

Willie stopped and steadied himself with his hand on the tree to his side.

Suddenly he thought he saw the shape move. He blinked. Maybe his eyes were playing tricks on him as they tried to recognize something familiar in the darkness.

A second time the shape seemed to move. Willie blinked again, and this time stepped a little closer to the tree, thinking he might hide behind it. But the dark shape held steady. The harder he stared, the less he could see until the shadow seemed to disappear altogether.

Then it moved again . . . and this time there was no mistake. It was moving, and it was coming toward him.

Soon he could even make out its feet, taking one step at a time. He could see its body and shoulders as though they were wrapped in a great coat. But . . . there was no head!

It looked like a headless man walking right toward him!

Willie's heart pounded harder and harder as he tried to tell himself that there was no such thing as a walking headless man, and yet, at that moment, he was watching one coming his way. Every nerve in his body wanted to flee, and yet he held his ground. He did not believe in ghosts and phantoms, and so he was not going to run away from something just because it looked like one.

But *something* was coming toward him. In fact, while blinking his eyes and hoping it would disappear, he heard the specter's feet crunching on dry grass and twigs. Not only his eyes but now his ears told him something was coming.

And then, when the phantom was no more than a few yards away, it raised its head . . . and he saw with great relief that it was not a headless man but an old horse that had simply been grazing its way through the cemetery with its head to the ground.

That old horse did not fool young Willie Seymour, and years later when magicians and con artists tried to fake God's miracles, Seymour was not easily fooled.

It seems like every time God does a great work by His Spirit, con artists try to gain fame and take people's money by performing a counterfeit. Frank Bartleman, one of the white leaders who assisted William Seymour, wrote, "We had the most to fear from the working of evil spirits within. Even spiritualists and hypnotists came to investigate and to try their influence. Then all the religious soreheads and crooks and cranks came seeking a place in the work. We had the most to fear from these."

Pastor Seymour wisely and quietly "prayed" these trouble causers into silence. He knew that if he drew too much attention to the devil's activities, the people would become afraid. They might fear that their free forms of worship and their exercise of spiritual gifts did not come from the Holy Spirit but from some evil spirit.

Bartleman claims that many times when someone got up to disrupt the meetings, "Their minds would wander, their brains reeling. Things would turn black before their eyes. They could not go on. I never saw one get by with it in those days. They were up against God. No one cut them off. We simply prayed. The Holy Spirit did the rest."

Discernment provides wisdom and safety
in frightening circumstances.

FROM GOD'S WORD:
Do not fear anything except the Lord Almighty. He alone is the Holy One. If you fear him, you need fear nothing else (Isaiah 8:13).

LET'S TALK ABOUT IT:
1. Why didn't William Seymour run when he thought he saw a headless man walking toward him?
2. Tell about a time when you were scared in the dark. What did you do?
3. How can fear cloud our judgment (discernment)? Think about the Bible verse from Isaiah 8:13. Why do we not need to fear anything other than God?

RECONCILIATION

Washing Away
the Color Line

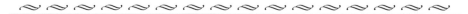

o! I won't allow a colored man in my classroom," said the teacher when William Seymour asked to attend his Bible school in Houston, Texas. "It's just not right to mix the races."

"But how can I learn about the Holy Spirit?" asked Seymour. "If what you say about a coming revival is true, I don't want to miss out."

"Well . . . well, you can sit outside the door in the hallway. Maybe you can hear a little there."

So that's how William Seymour attended Charles F. Parham's Bible school in 1905. Seymour had come to Houston a couple of years earlier to look for some relatives his family had lost track of during slavery. When he found them they invited him to live with them while he preached at various churches in the area.

One day he met a young black woman, Lucy Farrow, who worked as a governess for the Parham family. Parham traveled around the Midwest preaching, evangelizing, and running short-term Bible schools. "When we were in Topeka, Kansas," Miss Farrow said, "a woman named Agnes Ozman spoke in unknown tongues, and then I did, too. Brother Parham says this is the first evidence of a Pentecostal revival. You ought to attend his Bible school here in Houston. It could change your life and your preaching forever."

So, in spite of the disgrace of being banished to the hallway, Seymour sat and listened. Parham said that in the last days God would pour out His Holy Spirit with power similar to what happened at Pentecost in the book of Acts. Believers would speak in tongues, prophesy, heal the sick, and spread the Gospel as never before. Parham had not yet experienced this renewal himself, but he believed that it was coming. After studying the Bible for himself, Seymour agreed and began preaching the same thing.

He took this message with him when he moved to Los Angeles to serve as pastor of a small mission there, and after a month of "waiting" in prayer and Bible study, the little congregation was "filled with the Holy Ghost, and began to speak with other tongues," similar to what was described in Acts 2:4.

But Seymour did not accept racial separation. He believed that the real miracle on the Day of Pentecost was the Holy Spirit's outpouring of so much godly love that three thousand people from "every nation under heaven" accepted the Gospel. The unity Jesus prayed for in John 17 was dramatically realized between former enemies and strangers. To Seymour, the gift of tongues was a way of communicating that love. And so the love that could unite people—blacks and whites, people from India and China and South America—was what mattered. Jesus shed His blood to forgive our sins and to wash away all divisions, including the "color line."

Six months later Charles Parham came to visit the Azusa Street Mission, apparently intending to take over. In his first message, he declared, "God is sick to His stomach" at all the racial mixing. Later his wife explained, "In Texas, you know, the colored people are not allowed to mix with the white people." Parham was a full-fledged racist and later became an open supporter of the Ku Klux Klan. He drew away some white people to start a rival church, as did other white leaders over the years until the Pentecostal movement became largely divided into black and white denominations.

However, many years later in 1994 and again in 1997, leaders of the Pentecostal and Charismatic Churches of North America (PCCNA) pursued reconciliation. After repenting and exchanging apologies and forgiveness, white and black leaders from the Assemblies of God, the Church of God in Christ, the Church of God of Prophecy, and various independent Pentecostal and charismatic groups washed one another's feet and pledged to eliminate racism in their churches.

Racial reconciliation helps fulfill Jesus' prayer in
John 17:11 that we all be made one.

FROM GOD'S WORD:
Christ . . . made [all races] one people. They were separated as if there were a wall between them, but Christ broke down that wall of hate by giving his own body (Ephesians 2:14, NCV).

LET'S TALK ABOUT IT:
1. What do you think Charles Parham feared if he let black people sit with whites in his classroom?
2. Which two people should be closer to each other, a black Christian and a white Christian, or two relatives of the same race where one is a Christian and one is not?
3. Since Jesus prayed that we would all be made one, how can you obey His will when you meet a Christian from another race?

FAITHFULNESS
Many Languages, Many Gifts, One Gospel

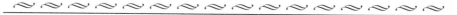

n the day Christians were first baptized by the Holy Spirit, we are told in Acts 2 that three thousand people believed. Many of these were foreigners who heard the Christians speaking in "tongues"—their own language. Later in the New Testament it appears that speaking in tongues served other purposes as well, such as praising God (Acts 10:46) or prophesying (1 Corinthians 14:6).

At William Seymour's Azusa Street Mission, spreading the Gospel was just as important as it was to the first Christians, and just like the New Testament believers, they sometimes used their gift of tongues to do it.

Sister Anna Hall visited a Russian church in Los Angeles and, by the power of the Holy Spirit, spoke to them in their own language. They were so glad that they wept and kissed her hand. They visited the Azusa Mission a few nights later when Brother Lee was empowered by the Spirit to speak and sing in their language. The Holy Spirit then fell on the Russian believers, and they, too, began glorifying God.

On August 10, 1906, on their way to Jerusalem as missionaries,

Andrew Johnson, Louise Condit, and Lucy Leatherman stopped in Oakland, California. They had been selected as missionaries because they had received several Middle Eastern languages. While in Oakland they were talking on the street about the gift of tongues, when Lucy Leatherman began speaking in tongues just as a man wearing a Turkish fez came by. He stopped and listened and then said in English, "You obviously are American, but in what university did you learn Turkish?"

When she explained that it was a gift from God, he was amazed. "I am from the university in Constantinople, but yours is the most perfect Turkish I have heard spoken by a foreigner."

She laughed and said, "Then you may not understand why I do not know what I have just said. Could you interpret for me?"

He did, and they continued speaking about the Gospel of Jesus Christ.

Some time later Lucy Farrow went on a short-term mission to West Africa and was enabled by the Holy Spirit to preach two sermons in the Kru language to the residents of Johnsonville, twenty-five miles south of Monrovia. Many accepted Christ and received the Holy Spirit, speaking in other tongues, some in English that Miss Farrow could understand perfectly.

Similar experiences followed dozens of missionaries from the Azusa Street Mission, who were sent all over the world—to India, China, Africa, Japan, Sweden, Ireland, Egypt, Palestine, and elsewhere. However, the ability to speak in a *specific* foreign tongue did not seem to be a permanent gift for most missionaries. "Tongues" became more and more an expression of prayer and praise and prophecy as we see happened in the latter portion of the New Testament.

Why wasn't it a permanent gift for these missionaries? Possibly the Lord used that particular gift to get the missionaries on the field and to get the work started. But then most had to buckle down to the hard task of learning the language of the people in order to carry on the work.

No matter what spiritual gift God gives us, we should use it faithfully.

Faithfulness helps us use spiritual gifts in a way that builds up the church and spreads the Gospel.

FROM GOD'S WORD:
God has given gifts to each of you from his great variety of spiritual gifts. Manage them well so that God's generosity can flow through you (1 Peter 4:10).

LET'S TALK ABOUT IT:
1. What was the purpose behind speaking in tongues and the use of other spiritual gifts at the Asuza Street Mission?
2. Why do you think the Russian-Americans responded so gladly when they heard someone from the Azusa Street Mission sharing the Gospel in Russian?
3. Make a list of all the "spiritual gifts" you can find in the New Testament (1 Corinthians 12:4–11; Ephesians 4:11). What spiritual gift(s) has God given you? How can you use your gift faithfully?

JOHN & BETTY STAM

They Lived—and Died—for Christ

Betty Scott couldn't help but notice the tall, good-looking young man in the "Prayer Meeting for China" at Moody Bible Institute in 1930. Born Elizabeth Alden Scott (her middle name hinted of her famous *Mayflower* ancestors, John and Priscilla Alden), Betty had been raised in China by missionary parents, and her heart still called it home. But what was John Stam's interest in China?

A year younger than Betty Scott, John Stam had also been raised in a devout Christian home dedicated to missions—on the home front. His immigrant parents had founded the Star of Hope Mission in Paterson, New Jersey, where many of Paterson's poor found not only food and comfort, but also hope and forgiveness by trusting Jesus Christ as Savior and Lord. The two young people found they had much in common: a zest for life, a love for people, a desire to serve God one hundred percent, and a call to missions. But even though they had fallen in love, Christ and His call on their lives came first. An official engagement would have to "wait and see."

Betty was accepted as a missionary candidate by China Inland Missions (CIM) and sailed for China in the fall of 1931. Graduating from Moody a year later, John was also accepted as a missionary candidate by CIM. Betty was waiting to meet him in Shanghai, China. *Now* they could move forward in serving God *together*.

But their year of engagement still meant separation. John plunged into language study in Anking, in southeast Anhwei Province, while Betty had been temporarily assigned to Fowyang, in northwest Anhwei Province. Both knew that a life in China would be full of uncertainties, not the least of which was an anti-Christian movement, fueled by Communist forces battling Nationalist forces, that threatened both Chinese Christians and foreign missionaries alike.

At last! A Western-style wedding in Shanghai on October 25, 1933, a honeymoon in Tsingtao, where Betty had grown up, and a temporary assignment to Suancheng under the oversight of veteran missionaries Mr. and Mrs. George Birch. Several walking mission trips in the mountainous province took them to outstations to encourage small groups of Chinese Christians. And then, on September 11, 1934, a child was born, Helen Priscilla Stam.

Baby Helen's young parents were thrilled to finally receive their assignment: to open a mission station in Tsingteh. Rumors were flying that Communist forces were advancing, but local magistrates promised protection for the foreigners. So with hearts full of praise, the young missionaries arrived in Tsingteh and began making friends with their Chinese neighbors.

The Stams had been in Tsingteh only a few weeks when the city was routed in a surprise attack by Communists on December 7, 1934. The following day, following a ten-mile march to Miaoshao, John and Betty Stam were executed with the sword. By a miracle of God's grace, baby Helen was spared . . . only the first of many miracles to sprout from these two "seeds" that fell into the ground and died.

PRAISE

Letters Home

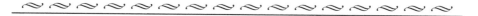

t was hard to get into a good grump around John Stam. The fellow had the delightful ability—or annoying habit, depending on your point of view—to see God at work in the most difficult situation, and he had the nerve to praise God for the smallest blessing even when surrounded by hardship.

While his classmates at Moody Bible Institute in the early 1930s were grumbling about all the homework they had to do, John added several small jobs to his study load just to make ends meet. Instead of complaining, he wrote to his father, Peter Stam: *"The Lord has wonderfully shown himself to me as Jehovah-jireh [the Lord will provide]. . . . How I do thank Him for this past year! I would not have had it otherwise for all the ease of a bank balance."*

John had already finished college when he decided to go to Moody Bible Institute to prepare for Christian service in China. Like any normal twenty-three-year-old, he hoped someday to meet "the girl of his dreams" . . . but probably wondered whether *any* girl would want to share a life of hardship on the mission field. He could hardly believe the goodness of God when he was introduced to Betty Scott, a sweet-faced girl with a friendly, outgoing nature who had grown up in China as a "missionary kid" and had already been accepted by China Inland Mission. The only hitch: She was sailing for China in September of 1931—and he hadn't even finished Moody yet, much less been accepted by CIM as a missionary!

He swallowed the urge to ask her to marry him and let her go. But he didn't sulk. If *God* wanted them together, God would work it out.

When John finally learned that he had been accepted by CIM and would sail for China on the *Empress of Japan* in late summer of 1932, he finally wrote Betty the letter he had written a thousand times in his mind: Would she marry him so together they could serve God as husband and wife in China?

But he had received no reply by the time the *Empress* sailed. Naturally John was a little worried. Had Betty changed her mind?

But when the *Empress* pulled into Shanghai harbor, John was overjoyed to find Betty waiting to meet him. His letter had gone to the wrong address but had finally caught up to her. Not only that, but she had come to Shanghai to meet her parents, who were returning from furlough, but they had been delayed—so she was still there when John arrived. And her answer was . . . *yes.*

Another letter sailed home to Paterson, New Jersey, by return ship: *"I still cannot cease praising the Lord and wondering at His goodness in bringing Betty to Shanghai and keeping her there until I came! . . . To me it has been a wonderful illustration of the fact that when we do 'seek first' the kingdom of God, although our efforts may be blundering, He does faithfully add the 'all things.' "*

John could hardly contain his joy after only two days of wedded bliss. He decided to write a letter to his parents *"on some typewriter around here, before our blessings pile up so high that I may forget some of them."* The honeymoon was short-lived, however, and the young couple found themselves plunged once more into language study and sharing meals with the Birches, an older missionary couple in Suancheng. Not exactly the privacy most newlyweds desire, but John wrote, *"I do thank the Lord for bringing me to this [mission] station, for there are many fine Christians here. . . ."*

A year later, John and Betty were settling into their first real mission assignment: the city of Tsingteh in the southeast corner of Anhwei Province. In spite of rumors of Communist aggression, in spite of the fact that twenty-seven Protestant missionaries had been killed in China in the past ten years (1924–1934), in spite of isolation—no cars, no telephones—John wrote to his parents, *"We do praise the Lord for the privilege of being here."* And on December 5, 1934: *"Things are always happening otherwise than one expects . . . [but] The Lord helps us to be quite satisfied, whatever He sends our way."*

Two days later that "satisfaction in the Lord" was put to the test. . . .

Praise is not dependent on changing circumstances, but knowing that in all circumstances, God is good.

FROM GOD'S WORD:
The Lord is good to all. . . . Everything you have made will praise you (Psalm 145:9–10, NIV).

LET'S TALK ABOUT IT:
1. Why do you think John Stam was so ready to praise God for everything?
2. What is the hardest thing you have ever faced? Can you find something to praise God for in that situation?
3. Have you praised God today for anything? It's not too late.

TRUST

"We're Going to Heaven"

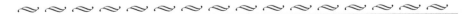

Three-month-old Helen Priscilla giggled and splashed in the wooden bucket of warm water that served as her bathtub. "Look, John," laughed Betty Stam, holding tight to her slippery daughter. "Helen thinks this is great fun."

Loud knocking interrupted the early-morning bath time in the China Inland Mission house in Tsingteh, Anhwei Province. Betty heard her husband go to the door, followed by a babble of high-pitched voices in Chinese. "Hide! Hide!"

Wrapping baby Helen in a towel, Betty hurried into the main room. "John? What is it?"

John Stam turned to his wife, concern in his gray eyes. "Communist soldiers . . . they've captured the city. All means of escape have been cut off."

Betty could hear people running and screaming in the street. She clutched the squirming baby to her chest. "We must pray—it is our only hope."

The young missionary couple called their two frightened Chinese helpers and knelt in prayer. While they were still praying, soldiers in the uniforms of the Red Army burst into the house. The head soldier demanded money and jewelry. While John tried to comply with their demands, Betty brought out a tray of hot tea and cakes and offered them to the soldiers. But the soldiers were angry at the small amount of money John was able to come up with. They tied John's hands and took him away; shortly they returned for Betty and the baby.

The soldiers allowed John to write a letter to China Inland Mission explaining their demand for $20,000 in ransom. The letter was dated December 6, 1934, and ended with the words, " . . . *as for us, may God be glorified whether by life or by death."*

Panic and chaos reigned in the city. The soldiers looted and killed many outright; others were taken captive. Six thousand strong, the Red Army evacuated the next morning, marching the captives over the mountains to their next destination: Miaosheo. John and Betty knew the Wang family, Christians in the town, but didn't dare contact them. But the local postmaster recognized them and cried out: "Where are you going?"

A slight smile crossed John's face. "I don't know where they're going," he called back, "but we're going to heaven!"

The second night of their captivity, the little missionary family was locked in a bedroom of the house of a rich man who had fled Miaosheo. John was tied to a bedpost, unable to move. Betty was left free to tend to the baby as best she could. Knowing that death could come at any moment, the newlyweds comforted each other. At least they were together. And nothing could happen unless God allowed it. Their greatest concern was little Helen. Oh, how they longed to protect her. But God knew. . . .

Dawn was barely breaking over the mountains when the soldiers marched back into the house. They ordered John and Betty to leave the baby and come with them. Quickly Betty bundled the baby warmly and laid her in the middle of the big bed. With a last tender look, her hands were bound and she was pushed after her husband.

The young couple was led through the streets as the soldiers jeered the "foreigners" and called the townspeople to come witness their execution. A man they recognized—a believer—pushed out of the crowd and begged the soldiers to let them go. They ignored him and took the Stams to a hillside out of town. Again the man begged for their lives, this time on his knees. The soldiers laughed. "Are you a Christian, too?" they jeered. The man was promptly arrested and led away.

It was over in a few moments. John was pushed to his knees; a sword flashed. Betty fell to her knees beside him. The sword again whistled through the air.

The soldiers thought that was the end of that. They left two hated foreigners crumpled in the dirt. But John and Betty Stam were already meeting their Savior in heaven . . . and their testimony was swelling like a tidal wave across the world.

*Trust in God's sovereignty can bring peace
even in the face of death.*

FROM GOD'S WORD:
I trust in God. I will not be afraid. What can people do to me? (Psalm 56:11, NCV).

LET'S TALK ABOUT IT:
1. What did John and Betty Stam know about death that their captors didn't know?
2. Why can we trust God even when our lives are in danger?
3. How can you develop the kind of trust in God that results in peace, not panic?

VICTORY
Baby in a Rice Basket

≈≈≈≈≈≈≈≈≈≈≈≈≈≈≈≈≈≈≈≈≈≈≈

The Red Army pulled out of Miaosheo and camped about three miles away. Under cover of darkness a little group of Chinese Christian refugees crept back into town to the home of the Wangs. The house had been looted, but that was the least of the Wangs' concerns. While in the hills they had heard a rumor that two foreigners, a husband and wife, had been executed by the Communists. That had to be their American friends, John and Betty Stam from Tsingteh! But . . . was the rumor true? And what about their baby girl?

Evangelist Lo spoke up. "I will see what I can find out." Leaving his wife and little son at the Wangs', Lo made his way around the town, quietly asking questions. The frightened people hurried on or pretended not to hear. Maybe the army had left spies in the town.

Lo was just about to give up his search when an old woman pulled on his sleeve. "I heard a baby cry," she whispered in his ear. "Up there." And she pointed to a big deserted house.

The house had been ransacked. Lo searched room after room, but all he found were signs that the Red Army had bunked there. He listened. All was still. With heavy heart, he turned to leave. And then he heard it.

The muffled wail of a tiny baby.

He followed the sound. There in the middle of a big bed lay a small sleeping bag. Inside was a very angry baby, waving her little fist. Hardly daring to breathe, the Chinese evangelist picked up the baby and held her close. He was holding a miracle.

Inside the bag Lo found evidence of a mother's love: a clean gown, several diapers, and two five-dollar bills pinned to the clothes.

But where were Helen Priscilla's parents? A few more questions, and Lo came upon the scene of the tragedy just outside the town—two bodies still lying in a pool of their own blood. The baby had been alone on the bed for a day and a half.

Hurrying back to the Wangs with his precious bundle, Lo reported all he had seen. Plans were quickly made: The Wangs would find a way to bury the bodies of John and Betty Stam; Lo and his wife would try to smuggle the baby to safety.

Using the money Betty Stam had pinned to the baby clothes, Lo found a man willing to carry two large rice baskets over the mountains. Inside one was the Los' four-year-old son, sick from exposure and dehydration. Inside the other was tiny Helen Priscilla Stam.

In villages along the way, Mrs. Lo found Chinese women willing to nurse the motherless child for a small fee. Finally in a larger town they were able to buy a tin of Lactogen, a nursing formula. Now Mrs. Lo was able to put baby Helen on a regular feeding schedule.

Five days later Mr. and Mrs. Lo stumbled into the yard of the China Inland Mission house in Suancheng. Mr. Birch, an American missionary, opened the door. Mrs. Lo handed him the bundle in her arms. "This is all we have left," she said brokenly.

Confused, Mr. Birch uncovered the face of the sleeping child. His eyes widened. Only a month or so earlier, he had dedicated Helen Priscilla to God in a special Sunday service when John and Betty Stam stopped in Suancheng on their way to their mission in Tsingteh. Overcome with both grief and joy, he wept.

Helen Priscilla Stam was taken to a hospital, where she was pronounced in perfect health, then delivered safely to her missionary grandparents, Dr. and Mrs. C. E. Scott. After hearing the news of John and Betty's death, her other grandparents in New Jersey received a telegram from a friend: *"Remember, you gave John to God, not to China."*

Jesus said, "Unless a kernel of wheat falls to the ground and dies, it remains only a single seed. But if it dies, it produces many seeds" (John 12:24, NIV). Hearing about the martyrdom of John and Betty Stam during a memorial service at Moody Bible Institute, seven hundred students stood to their feet to give their lives to missionary service.

Victory knows that nothing can separate us from the love of God, and even death can result in new life.

FROM GOD'S WORD:
Death, where is your victory? Death, where is your pain? . . . But we thank God! He gives us the victory through our Lord Jesus Christ (1 Corinthians 15:55, NCV).

LET'S TALK ABOUT IT:
1. How did John and Betty Stam experience victory even though they were killed by the Communists?
2. What do you think the telegram to John's parents meant: *"Remember, you gave John to God, not to China"*?
3. What does "victory through our Lord Jesus Christ" mean to you?

TOM WHITE

A Really "Bad" Bible Boy

Tom White didn't plan to go to prison, but he couldn't let go of what he'd learned about Christians suffering for their faith. In the 1970s officials from Communist countries were telling the world that they allowed religious freedom. But Tom kept learning that many Christians in those countries were beaten, imprisoned, or even killed for preaching the Gospel.

Russian and Cuban pastors coming to the Free World on *official* tours sometimes claimed to enjoy complete freedom. But they never brought their families, and they evaded direct questions about Christians imprisoned for their faith or Bibles that had been confiscated or churches that had been closed or destroyed by the government.

The more Communist officials—and even some church officials in the United States—claimed that there was religious freedom in these countries, the more the reports of oppression and persecution increased. Tom met with Cuban refugees, and the stories were consistent—even from unbelievers: The government did everything possible to stamp out Christianity.

Why didn't more Americans know this? "Westerners truly want to believe the best of people," Tom White concluded. "While this is an admirable trait, when carried to the extreme, it becomes willful ignorance."

So Tom committed himself to two tasks: supporting persecuted Christians around the world and letting the Free World know about their suffering.

Cuba was not far away, and Christians there needed gospel literature, so Tom joined with other Christians to provide it. To get the Gospel to the people in a country where distributing Christian literature was prohibited, they packaged it in waterproof plastic baggies and dropped thousands of them into the sea off the coast of Cuba so that the ocean currents would carry them ashore. Later, Tom made flights over Cuba, dropping similar packets from a plane, distributing over four hundred thousand pieces of Christian literature.

But on May 27, 1979, his small plane crash-landed in Cuba after he finished a night drop. He and his pilot were arrested, interrogated (under torture), and sentenced to twenty-four years in prison.

After three months in solitary confinement, Tom was moved into the main prison population of seven thousand, where he met and worshiped with many members of the Cuban church who were imprisoned for their faith.

Extensive prayer and international appeals from U.S. Congressmen, Mother Teresa, and others finally secured Tom and his pilot's release after only seventeen months in prison.

Upon returning to the United States, Tom White became the director of The Voice of the Martyrs, an organization that encourages and supports persecuted Christians around the world. The Voice of the Martyrs has identified over forty countries where persecution of Christians is overlooked or even encouraged by the government. While not officially condoned, persecution of Christians occurs in many other locations around the world, as well. According to a Regent University study, some 156,000 Christians were martyred in 1995, more than in the entire first century.

SELF-SACRIFICE

Just One More Trip

~~~~~~

Tom White made his first trip to deliver Christian literature to people in Cuba in the winter of 1972. He arranged for a fishing boat to sail along the coast where he and others dumped fifty thousand watertight plastic packets into the sea to be washed ashore. They prayed that people would find them and read about Jesus.

Less than a year later he planned to make a run with twice as many packets, but the boat was unavailable so he found someone who could fly him to Cuba. Accidentally, they dropped part of their load over land rather than into the sea. Two MIG fighter planes threatened them for a time, but later, as they considered what had happened, they felt it was all in God's plan: Probably more people received the literature.

In December 1973 Tom got married. During this time he taught at a Christian school on Grand Cayman Island in the Caribbean Sea. His ministry was expanding. A year and a half later, he and his wife had their first child. Life was full steam ahead.

Suddenly he became extremely weak and pale. At the hospital the doctor discovered massive internal bleeding. Tom had been working too hard and was too weak for an operation. Gradually, however, the bleeding stopped, and after weeks of rest, he regained enough strength for him and his family to move to California, where he went to work for a mission agency that helped Christians in Communist countries.

Only a tiny percentage of these Christians were able to flee, but from them Tom heard firsthand stories of suffering and persecution. Even his own minister, Dr. Juan Oropesa, had spent seven years in Fidel Castro's prison because of his faith. Other refugees spoke of how much they longed for portions of the Bible. Tom wanted to help.

He remembered his "accidental drop" over land two years earlier. Why not do it again?

But before he could formulate a plan, Tom began vomiting blood one day while driving down a Los Angeles freeway. While looking for an exit ramp to get safely off the highway, he passed out and crashed his car. In the hospital the doctors operated and found several things wrong, including cancer.

Tom's long recovery, however, gave him time to plan the next drop. There *was* a permissible way to fly across Cuba if they stayed in the narrow flight corridor en route to Jamaica. If they went at night, they could drop literature, hopefully without being detected until daylight, when they would be safely gone. He ordered a hundred thousand copies of literature and engaged Christian pilots John Lessing and Linda Jackson.

With Tom still so weak he could hardly lift the five-pound packets of literature, they made a successful drop of half of the literature on December 7, 1976, saving the remainder for another flight.

But before Tom could make a second trip, he had another bleeding episode. It was the cancer again, but this time the surgeon was able to remove it. While in recovery, Tom prayed, "Oh, God, what do I do? It is physically impossible for me to continue this work."

Then the Holy Spirit reminded him of Philippians 4:13, "I can do all things through Christ who strengthens me" (NKJV).

"O dear God," Tom said, "give me one more trip, just one more trip."

Sacrificing yourself for others follows Christ's example.

FROM GOD'S WORD:

So brothers and sisters, since God has shown us great mercy, I beg you to offer your lives as a living sacrifice to him (Romans 12:1a, NCV).

LET'S TALK ABOUT IT:

1. Why did Tom White want to drop literature to the Cuban people?
2. Why do you think he didn't give up his idea even though he became very sick?
3. What kind of sacrifices are you willing to make to do something God is asking you to do?

FAITH

"Mayday! Mayday! We're Going Down!"

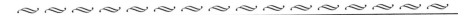

The small plane bucked and stumbled through the rough night air as it strained toward the lightning-laced thunderheads. "We've got to go around," yelled the pilot, Mel Bailey, over the roar of the engine.

"But look at our gas." Tom White's hand floated up and down and side to side as he tried to point to the gas gauges. "We'll never make it!"

Having just crossed over Cuba, they were heading toward Jamaica. But their time over Cuba had been far more than the most direct path from Florida to Jamaica. While Mel guided the plane through the night sky on May 27, 1979, Tom had dumped seventeen boxes of Christian literature out the door. Thousands and thousands of tracts fluttered to the ground to be picked up by people who had never heard about Jesus in this country where the Communist government opposed the Gospel.

But the plane no sooner turned away from the face of the thunderclouds than its navigational equipment stopped working. Tom and Mel flew on through the dark night until, rising out of a sea shimmering in the lightning, they could make out what looked like the dark mass of an island. Mel began calling on the radio to the airport in Montego Bay for instructions. The airport controllers said they were flashing their runway lights, but the only lights Tom and Mel saw on the ground remained steady and looked like the lights of villages, not a runway.

Suddenly the engine sputtered and died—out of gas.

"Montego," said Mel into his microphone, "we're heading toward some lights, coming straight in."

"Roger," said the controller. "We'll send out the fire trucks, but we still haven't spotted you visually or on radar."

As Mel and Tom continued to descend, there were fewer and fewer options. "There," Tom said, pointing through the dark. "I think that's a highway. Let's land on it."

Mel banked the plane and squinted at the road illumined by the lights from occasional houses and streetlights. "There? But there's people along it."

"They'll get out of the way when they see we are in trouble and coming in."

Again, Mel grabbed the mike. "Mayday. Mayday. Mayday. We're going in on a country road, but I don't know where! Mayday!"

Mel then concentrated on guiding the plane to a perfect landing on the narrow road.

With the wheels still about a foot off the ground, Tom raised his hand in warning, but it was too late. The right wing smashed into a dump truck that was parked to the side. The plane spun around, then twisted and tumbled down the road for four hundred yards until it screeched to a stop upside down.

Amazingly, neither Tom nor Mel was injured or even bruised, but when they climbed out of the plane, they discovered that the people who came running up all spoke Spanish.

They were in Cuba, not Jamaica!

Within moments the G–2 police came racing through the crowd

and arrested Tom and Mel. Would they be thrown in prison or tortured or shot? Who would know where they were? How could anyone help them?

"Well," said Tom to Mel as they waited to see what would happen to them, "the King of the universe was riding with us when we crashed. He'll continue to be with us even in Cuba. Just hang on to Him and take each moment as it comes."

Faith is hanging on to Jesus when all else seems lost.

FROM GOD'S WORD:

Let us look only to Jesus, the One who began our faith and who makes it perfect (Hebrews 12:2a).

LET'S TALK ABOUT IT:

1. Why do you think Tom White thought it was so important to get the Gospel to people in Cuba?
2. Why did Tom and Mel have faith that God would take care of them after they were arrested?
3. Can you think of any people who took a great risk or paid a high price to make the Bible available to us? Tell how.

PRAISE
"I'm Just Singing About Jesus!"

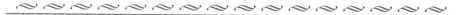

Well, well, Thomas," said the smartly dressed officer. "I guess you know that your mission failed this time. You got away last year, but now we have you. Total failure!"

Tom White noticed the gospel tract in the captain's hand. "Captain, we may have crashed on your island, but we didn't fail. All of the literature was distributed. I really don't care what you do to me. Are you going to shoot me?"

"No. We're not going to shoot you. Nothing so final." He looked at the tract in his hand. "But we *will* find all this literature."

Tom shrugged his thin shoulders. "The fact that you have even one piece shows me that my mission has not failed."

The captain frowned and read it again while Tom smiled inside. One more person was hearing the Gospel. He could not help saying, "You know, Jesus gives me great peace even now as I sit here in front of you."

Suddenly the door burst open and a major stomped into the room. "Stop this Jesus talk," he shouted, waving his hands. "You're with the CIA!"

The Cubans did not shoot Tom, but in the weeks to come they did their best to make him wish he were dead. "Your family has forgotten you. They think you are dead," they said. When the food they gave him made him sick, his captors tried to scare him by saying, "You're not looking too good, Tom. I think your cancer's coming back."

They put a hood over his head and drove him around as though they were taking him to some far location and then threw him into a refrigerated cell with no windows. Soon his teeth were chattering with cold.

"Now will you tell us who you work for?" Fidel Castro's officials asked Tom at the next questioning.

"I work for Jesus!"

On and on they questioned him until Tom stopped answering and started praying silently for his captors: *Oh, God, help Antonio. Break through, Jesus. He is the one in the cold, for he has never felt the warmth of your love.*

"What are you doing?" demanded the captain.

"I'm praying for you."

Tom's answer stunned the officer. Finally he screamed, "Do you think this is a game? You are going to be sorry!"

Back in the deep freeze, Tom started praying for every church he had ever attended and every Christian he could remember. Then he sang "A Mighty Fortress Is Our God" and "Jesus Loves Me" and every other Christian song he could recall.

"What are you doing?" yelled a guard through the little hole in the steel door.

"I'm just singing about Jesus!"

"Why?"

"Because I love Him."

"Well, stop!"

But Tom wouldn't stop. It was his source of strength.

In spite of being given a twenty-four-year sentence, Tom's captors told him on October 13, 1980, that he was to be released. Was it true? Would he go home after only seventeen months in prison? Three times Tom and Mel were taken through fake releases only to be marched back to their cells, their hopes smashed.

Tom remembered the song he sang at his baptism years before: "Where He Leads Me I Will Follow." He chewed on those words in his mind, swallowed them, believed them. Affirming that God—not his Communist captors—was in control helped him survive their cruel games.

Finally, two weeks after the official announcement, Tom and Mel actually boarded a plane and returned to the United States as free men.

Praising God reminds us He is good,
all-powerful, and loves us.

FROM GOD'S WORD:
Praise him for his acts of power; praise him for his surpassing greatness. . . . Let everything that has breath praise the Lord (Psalm 150:2, 6, NIV).

LET'S TALK ABOUT IT:
1. How do you think the captain felt when Tom was praying for him?
2. Why did Tom sing while in prison?
3. How can praising God help when you are scared? Have you tried it?

WILLIAM WILBERFORCE

British Antislavery Crusader

On August 24, 1759, William Wilberforce was born into a wealthy English family, but he was so weak and puny that he later joked that in a less-civilized time he would not have survived. But survive he did to become a real fighter, not only for himself but for the end of the British slave trade and of slavery itself in the British colonies.

When William was nine, his father died. Because his mother couldn't care for him, he went to live with relatives, where he received a fine early education and regularly attended a church where John Newton was an occasional guest speaker. (Newton was the former slave-trading captain who repented, gave his life to Christ, and later wrote the hymn "Amazing Grace." See *Hero Tales II*.)

Later, William returned to live with his mother in the city of Kingston upon Hull, where he ignored most of his religious training and busied himself attending plays and parties. Even though he spent little time studying, he was very bright and at the age of fourteen wrote a newspaper article against slavery—possibly reflecting some of the ideas he had heard from John Newton.

However, instead of studying when he went off to Cambridge

University, Wilberforce occupied himself playing cards and socializing. He was as good a speaker as he was a writer and soon got the idea that he ought to run for public office. When he turned twenty-one, he was elected to the House of Commons but only *after* spending nearly £9,000 on the election. Even as a member of Parliament, though, he spent most of his time gambling and drinking and having parties.

Wilberforce climbed high in social circles, accompanying his friend William Pitt (who had just been named prime minister) on holiday to Paris, where they were invited into the court of Louis XVI and Marie Antoinette. Later, the French people revolted against this king and queen, overthrowing and finally beheading them. But on this occasion Wilberforce had a high old time, partying day and night.

On his next two holidays Wilberforce returned to France, but with Isaac Milner, his former tutor, who was only eight years his senior. On their second trip, Milner brought a devotional book by Philip Doddridge, an English clergyman, and soon Wilberforce and Milner were spending all their time discussing it. It was the tool God used to convict Wilberforce that he had been wasting his life in foolishness and sin.

On November 28, 1785, at age twenty-six, he repented and gave his life to Christ.

The Society of Friends (Quakers) in Britain had been campaigning against the slave trade for many years and had already approached Wilberforce for help. Before his conversion he couldn't be bothered, but when he returned to England, Wilberforce consulted John Newton about his life's direction. Newton advised him to remain in Parliament and work for justice, especially for slaves. This became Wilberforce's lifelong assignment from God. Even though he gained the help of many other people, including his old friend and prime minister, William Pitt, it wasn't until 1807 that the British slave trade was abolished.

William Wilberforce died on July 29, 1833, four days after Parliament finally passed the Emancipation Bill, abolishing slavery in all the British colonies.

TEACHABILITY

The Proud Man in the Dark Coat

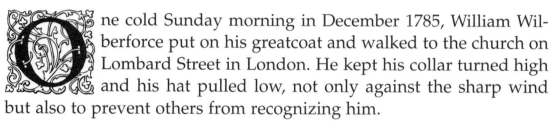

One cold Sunday morning in December 1785, William Wilberforce put on his greatcoat and walked to the church on Lombard Street in London. He kept his collar turned high and his hat pulled low, not only against the sharp wind but also to prevent others from recognizing him.

After hearing a powerful sermon by John Newton in St. Mary's Church, William remained in his pew until nearly everyone had left. Then he approached the old preacher and withdrew an envelope from inside his coat.

"Sir, allow me to give you this. It is of great importance." Then he put on his hat and went back out into the freezing air.

The letter in the envelope, signed by William Wilberforce, asked Newton for a secret meeting to discuss important matters. Even without the coat, Newton wouldn't have recognized the visitor, for he hadn't seen William since he was a ten-year-old.

Of course he would meet with Wilberforce! But why such secrecy?

The following Wednesday William again walked to Lombard Street rather than take a carriage in which he might be recognized. But when he got to Newton's house, he walked on past and then around and around the square. Would Newton laugh at him? Finally he gathered his courage and went to the door.

Newton greeted him warmly. The two men talked about old times, about William's successful rise in Parliament, about Newton's preaching and songwriting. Finally Newton said, "What brings you here today, William?"

William shifted in his chair. "In spite of my success, I have not been at peace, not until recently when God's Word came alive to me. Now I have truly repented of my wild and useless life, but I don't know what to do."

"What do you mean?" replied the former sea captain.

"What shall I do with my life? I know that Jesus told the rich young ruler to sell all he had and give it to the poor. Should I do that? Should I leave politics and become a preacher like you or John Wesley? I have quit gambling and drinking, but should I abandon fashionable society? I do want God to forgive me. Maybe I should become a monk and live in a monastery—"

"Do not doubt that your sins have been forgiven, William. Whatever you do, it is not to earn forgiveness if you repented sincerely. As for Parliament—" Newton paused and stroked his smooth-shaven chin—"God could have some important work for you there." He squinted thoughtfully, as though looking into the sunny glare of the sea. "What are your views on slavery?"

"I'm quite against it," said William, recalling an essay he had written against slavery as a youth. "But I haven't thought much about it lately. Why?"

"Go think about it, and then let's talk some more . . . maybe in a week or so?"

No longer concerned that someone might see him calling on the old preacher, William visited Newton often, seeking his wisdom until he gained a clear vision of God's plan for his life. He decided to join with the Quakers and others who opposed slavery and use his voice in Parliament to bring it to an end.

You have to be teachable before you can learn anything.

FROM GOD'S WORD:
Ask and it will be given to you; seek and you will find; knock and the door will be opened to you (Matthew 7:7, NIV).

LET'S TALK ABOUT IT:
1. Why do you think William Wilberforce needed John Newton's help?
2. Why do you think he at first wanted his meetings with Newton to be secret?
3. How can our pride affect whether we learn something?

ENDURANCE
John Wesley's Last Letter

ritain, the world's leader in all trade, had supplied over three million African slaves to the British colonies. Many people thought of slaves as no more than property. Once, for instance, when a ship ran into a bad storm while crossing the Atlantic, the captain threw 132 slaves overboard to lighten his load. When he finally got to England, he applied to his insurance company to pay for his "lost cargo"!

William Wilberforce worked closely with people like Thomas Clarkson to gather information about the cruelties of slavery to convince Parliament to end the evil trade. He even made a model of a slave ship to demonstrate how the slaves were transported—shelves only three or four feet high where men, women, and children were "stacked" and chained together two by two.

When John Newton came and testified to the Privy Council Committee on his experiences as a slave captain, he broke down and cried as he described the part he had played in that cruel trade.

It took three years, but finally Wilberforce was ready to present his antislavery bill to Parliament. But in March 1788 he became so ill his doctors feared he would die.

"Pitt," he said to his old friend the prime minister, "if I don't recover, will you introduce this bill against slavery for me?"

"Don't talk like that, dear fellow. You'll bounce back soon enough."

"But if I don't—?"

"Then I promise with all my heart. You can count on me," said Pitt.

From then on, Wilberforce began to recover, though it was months before he was back in London and ready to address Parliament. He made his first great speech on the subject on May 12, 1789. "God has commanded, 'You shall do no murder,' and yet our slave trade means the murder of thousands of Africans each year," he declared. He spoke for three and a half hours, but there were just too many politicians influenced by the rich slave traders, and the bill was defeated.

Wilberforce and his associates would have to try again.

But in July, angry mobs in France stormed the Bastille, and the possibility of a French revolution became the talk of London. England was already ruled by Parliament rather than the whim of a king or queen, so there was considerable sympathy in England for the cause of the French people. But who could know where a revolution might lead? It was not a good time to ask Parliament to consider the slave trade again.

How discouraging!

Then one day Wilberforce received a letter from John Wesley, the great preacher and founder of the Methodist movement. (See *Hero Tales I*.) Written on February 24, 1791, it said, "*Unless God has raised you up, humanly I don't see how you can go through with your glorious enterprise in opposing the villainous slave trade. You will be worn out by the opposition of men and devils. But if God is with you, who can be against you? Oh, be not weary in well-doing. Go on, in the name of God and in the power of His might till even American slavery, the vilest that ever saw the sun, shall banish away before it.*"

It was the last letter Wesley would ever write. The old gentleman died one week later. But his encouragement gave Wilberforce the strength to endure.

The French Revolution erupted, and the revolutionaries, drunk on the blood of their monarchs and nobles, swore to destroy kings everywhere, even declaring war on England in February 1793. So Wilberforce had to wait and work another fourteen years before the British slave trade was finally outlawed in 1807.

Love never gives up.

FROM GOD'S WORD:
Let us not become weary in doing good, for at the proper time we will reap a harvest if we do not give up (Galatians 6:9, NIV).

LET'S TALK ABOUT IT:
1. How do you think Wilberforce felt when he became sick just when he hoped to introduce the bill against the slave trade?
2. Both then and later, what encouraged him to endure?
3. Read Hebrews 12:12–13. How is endurance in doing right like a long race?

SHARING
A "Joshua" to Carry On

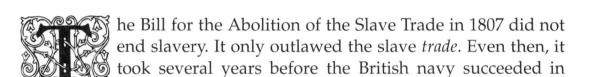

The Bill for the Abolition of the Slave Trade in 1807 did not end slavery. It only outlawed the slave *trade*. Even then, it took several years before the British navy succeeded in stopping British ships from transporting new slaves to America. But what about the slaves who still lacked freedom and were often cruelly treated?

William Wilberforce was growing old, and he needed to find someone to carry on his work the way Moses found Joshua.

"That's the man for me," said William when he heard Thomas Fowell Buxton speak on behalf of the poor at a London Mansion House meeting in 1816. "He has the kind of fire in him that will carry the day."

So, with Wilberforce's encouragement, Buxton entered Parliament a couple years later, and soon Wilberforce was giving him more and more responsibilities in the fight against slavery.

Meanwhile, Wilberforce wrote a booklet on the subject that gained wide popularity. But when it came time for a vote in Parliament on May 15, 1823, the best Buxton and Wilberforce could achieve was an amendment restricting cruelty to slaves, outlawing the whipping of women, for instance. These rules made the slaveholders in the colonies so angry that many chose to keep the rules secret from their slaves. When word got out, it was distorted to say that slavery had been abolished. Thinking they were being held in bondage unlawfully, some thirteen thousand slaves in British Guiana revolted.

Troops were called out and hundreds were killed. The rest were severely punished. Even a white missionary was falsely accused and convicted of encouraging the slave revolt. He died in prison.

Back in England, Wilberforce was blamed for all the trouble, and the cause of completely freeing British slaves was set back. Reluctantly, Wilberforce retired from Parliament in 1825 after serving forty-five years in the House of Commons.

But he did not give up. He kept working with Buxton and speaking—as his health allowed—at various antislavery rallies around the country. Slowly the cause gained momentum again, and with Buxton's careful guidance, the bill was reintroduced in 1833.

Unfortunately, the elderly Wilberforce was too ill to attend. A key ingredient was attached to the new bill. England as a nation had sponsored the slave trade, and even though the plantation owners now owned the slaves, the nation as a whole needed to accept responsibility to buy back the slaves' freedom.

On July 25, 1833, as old William Wilberforce lay dying on his bed in Cadogan Place, a messenger arrived from Buxton. "It has passed! It has passed, dear friend."

"Will the government pay compensation?" asked Wilberforce, concerned that the slave owners might revolt if their "property" was just taken away.

"Yes," said the messenger. "Twenty million pounds, to which the slave owners' representatives have agreed. The bill has passed, and in a year's time every slave in the empire will be free."

"Thank God," said the feeble voice from the bed. "And to think that I should live to witness the day on which England is willing to pay twenty million pounds of silver for the abolition of slavery!"

Four days later, Wilberforce died knowing that he had completed his assignment from God. At midnight on July 31, 1834, over a million slaves in the British colonies were set free.

Sharing includes responsibilities as well as benefits.

FROM GOD'S WORD:
Then I heard the voice of the Lord saying, "Whom shall I send? And who will go for us?" And I said, "Here am I. Send me!" (Isaiah 6:8, NIV).

LET'S TALK ABOUT IT:
1. Why was Wilberforce looking for someone like Joshua?
2. Why is it sometimes hard to share responsibilities?
3. Tell about a time when you and someone else shared in a task where others said, "Well done."

List of Character Qualities ⟊

ADVOCATE
   Windy-City Panhandler (Ricky and Sherialyn Byrdsong)

BOLDNESS
   A Wounded Head Under a Hairy Scalp (Joy Ridderhof)
   Angels Watching Over You (Rómulo Sauñe)

CARING
   Shepherd Through the Wilderness (Samson Occom)

COMPASSION
   A New Year's Celebration (Pandita Ramabai)

DEDICATION
   Passing Up the Good to Achieve the Best (John G. Paton)

DIGNITY
   "That's Not Fair!" (Samson Occom)

DIPLOMACY
   The Disinvited Guests (Pandita Ramabai)

DISCERNMENT
   The Headless Phantom (William J. Seymour)

ENCOURAGEMENT
   Snip and Stitch (Eliza Davis George)

ENDURANCE
   John Wesley's Last Letter (William Wilberforce)

FAITH
   "Mayday! Mayday! We're Going Down!" (Tom White)

FAITHFULNESS
   Many Languages, Many Gifts, One Gospel (William J. Seymour)

FORESIGHT
   Creating Our Own Settlements (Samson Occom)

DAVE AND NETA JACKSON are an award-winning husband-and-wife writing team, the authors or coauthors of over a hundred books. They are most well-known for the TRAILBLAZERS, a forty-book series of historical fiction about great Christian heroes for young readers (with sales topping 1.7 million), and Neta's popular *Yada Yada Prayer Group* novels for women.

Dave and Neta bring their love for historical research to the four-volume series of HERO TALES. Each book features fifteen Christian heroes, highlighting important character qualities through forty-five nonfiction stories from their lives.

The Jacksons make their home in the Chicago metropolitan area, where they are active in cross-cultural ministry and enjoy their grandchildren.

Around the World With Christian Heroes!

TRAILBLAZER BOOKS give you an adventure story, an introduction to a Christian hero of the past, and a look at a time and place that will fascinate you. Whatever country or time interests you most, chances are there's a TRAILBLAZER BOOK about it. And, each story is told through the eyes of a boy or girl your age. Be sure to travel the globe and go back through time with the TRAILBLAZER BOOKS.

TRAILBLAZER BOOKS by Dave and Neta Jackson

Ambushed in Jaguar Swamp – Grubb
The Bandit of Ashley Downs – Müller
Caught in the Rebel Camp – Douglass
The Chimney Sweep's Ransom – Wesley
Defeat of the Ghost Riders – Bethune
The Drummer Boy's Battle – Nightingale
Escape From the Slave Traders – Livingstone
Exiled to the Red River – Garry
The Fate of the Yellow Woodbee – Saint
The Forty-Acre Swindle – Carver
The Hidden Jewel – Carmichael
Hostage on the Nighthawk – Penn
Imprisoned in the Golden City – Judson
Journey to the End of the Earth – Seymore

Kidnapped by River Rats – Booth
Listen for the Whippoorwill – Tubman
The Mayflower Secret – Bradford
The Queen's Smuggler – Tyndale
Quest for the Lost Prince – Morris
Risking the Forbidden Game – Cary
Roundup of the Street Rovers – Brace
The Runaway's Revenge – Newton
Shanghaied to China – Taylor
Sinking the Dayspring – Paton
Spy for the Night Riders – Luther
The Thieves of Tyburn Square – Fry
Traitor in the Tower –Bunyan
Trial by Poison – Slessor

◊ BETHANYHOUSE